THE NEW YORK TIMES

BOOK
OF
HOUSE
PLANTS

by Joan Lee Faust

Illustrated by Allianora Rosse

Quadrangle

The New York Times Book Co.

THE NEW YORK TIMES

BOOK
OF
HOUSE
PLANTS

PHOTO CREDITS

Robert C. Baur 197
John Bickel 181
General Electric and Company 180
Gottscho-Schleisner 2, 11, 20, 47, 182, 185, 204, 209
John T. Hill 2
Riekes Crisa Corporation 198, 199
Roche 227
Ben Schnall, Designs for Business, Inc. 191
George Taloumis 8, 14, 17, 25, 41, 44, 47, 207, 211, 216, 222, 235
Nan Tucker 228
Mason Weymouth 190
Other photographs courtesy of The New York Times

Color illustrations by Allianora Rosse
Black and white illustrations by Harry Carter

Seventh Printing

Library of Congress Catalog Card Number: 72-91701
International Standard Book Number: 0-8129-0309-9

BOOK DESIGN BY BETTY BINNS

For Poppy

contents

appendix

THE NEW YORK TIMES

BOOK
OF
HOUSE
PLANTS

introduction

Plants in a house or an apartment help to make a home. Whether there are many in handsome pottery and planters or just a few humble pots of ivy, the presence of green leaves provides a feeling of warmth and hospitality.

The house plants grown today have been collected from all parts of the world by professionally trained botanists who are often called "plant hunters." They seek out unusual, beautiful species that will adapt readily to home temperatures.

The environment inside a house or apartment is obviously different from the climate in which these plants are "discovered." This point is important. For when plants are grown successfully indoors, they are being trained to grow in a people's climate. In other words, indoor plants are wild plants that have been domesticated.

For some of the better-known common house plants this domestication technique is quite well established. More challenging are the newer introductions being gleaned from

all parts of the world, particularly the tropical regions. Although a great deal is known about their indoor growing, new things are always being learned. Knowledge of a plant's natural habitat provides many helpful clues for growing it indoors successfully.

The majority of plants used for interior decor originally came from the tropic zones of Central and South America. Most grew at elevations where temperature fluctuates, a factor that makes these plants more adaptable to life indoors. Imagine the natural environment in which these plants grow: heavy rainfall and evaporation from streams and waterfalls providing bountiful humidity; the constant rotting away of cast-off plant leaves and fallen branches making the soil rich with humus; and thick vegetation giving plenty of shade. When these plants are grown indoors, they obviously need high humidity, humus-rich soil, and filtered light.

Cacti and succulents that grow in the desert regions of Central and North America are exposed to hot baking sun for long hours. The soil is thin and sandy. Rainfall is practically nil. In homes, these plants need little water, plenty of sunshine, and sandy soil.

Sometimes by their appearance plants offer strong clues about themselves—clues that provide a guide to their care. Consider the thick leaves of the jade plant, which came from semiarid areas in South Africa. These leaves are capable of storing water for dry seasons much as a cactus stores water. As a result, the jade plant requires water less frequently than the moisture-loving plants from the tropics.

In contrast, *Coleus* has thin foliage. Because

3

the leaves store little moisture, they wilt quickly when the plant is not supplied regularly with enough water.

Simple, practical observations like these will give anyone a better understanding of plant care. In time, the novice will begin to develop a natural "plant sense." As his confidence builds up, he will learn to relax about keeping plants and to enjoy them.

One other thing should be kept in mind. There is a limit to what anyone can do to help a plant grow. After all, the actual growing is up to the plant. Once accepted, this attitude dispels any "green thumb" or "brown thumb" complexes. In growing plants there is no special magic that some people have and others have not. By learning what is needed to maintain plants indoors, success is possible for everyone.

care of house plants

To grow, most plants need four simple elements—light, water, air, and soil. The temperature and humidity of the air are also important. In an environment where these needs are fully satisfied, plants thrive. But in a home environment, planned for people, greenery often falters. That is why it is important to acquire a basic understanding of how plants grow and what factors influence their growth. This knowledge, plus a good dose of common sense, will enable anyone to grow a surprising number of plants indoors.

In this book the basics of plant care are discussed under topical headings for easy reference. Undergraduates in the tending of house plants should read all topics carefully. Graduates can be excused from reading every word, but should refer to various sections as needed for brushups.

Selection of what plants to grow should be based on their appeal to the eye and their environmental needs. There is no point in taking home a plant whose light, temperature, and humidity requirements cannot be satisfied by the environment in your home. Nor is there any point in acquiring a plant that does not please with its leaf shape and colors. Select plants for their interesting appearance or decorative value. Although a collection of one-of-a-kind plants grouped together can be very effective, a collection of different kinds of plants is more fascinating for the grower.

light

How well plants grow depends on how much natural light reaches them. If shade trees and shrubs surround the home, their branches will cut down on the amount of light that enters the windows. A house next door will block light. And the direction in which a window faces will determine the quality of light coming through it.

Windowsills or window shelves are favorite places to grow plants, but, contrary to what many people think, direct sunlight is not always best for house plants. In fact, it may burn the foliage of some plants. Only plants that require intense light—plants such as *Cyclamen*, gardenia, geranium, waxplant, and others that are grown mainly for flowers—should be grown in full sunlight, which means a window facing south.

East or west windows, which receive morning or afternoon sun, suit African violet, flame violet, *Fatsia*, bromeliads, and many orchids. In windows receiving north light—that is, bright light but no direct sunlight—foliage

plants such as *Philodendron* should be grown.

So much for windowsill exposures. Accent plants used as part of interior decor do not have to be directly in front of windows to thrive, but the degree of light available to them should be a major consideration determining the plants selected. Bright light exposure, just beyond the reaches of the sun's rays, is suitable for most large, treelike, decorative plants— umbrella tree, figs, bamboo palm, and some ferns.

Where light intensity is low, some distance from a window, yet in a bright room, it is possible to raise *Dracaena,* dumb cane, snake plant, *Syngonium,* and *Philodendron.* But water such plants sparingly and give them fertilizer only infrequently. A minimum maintenance program will be more successful for keeping these plants alive than one that tends to force fast growth for which there is not enough light. Plants placed in dim light do best if they are helped to "exist" rather than grow.

In less than dim light—what might be called a dark apartment, either on a first floor or facing a small court—growing plants is a difficult uphill struggle. Not many interesting plants can be grown. Possibly the only candidates might be the ever durable *Sansevieria* or *Aspidistra.* People in dark apartments would find plant growing much more fun and interesting if they would follow the ideas for growing plants in artificial light, covered on pages 171 to 178.

No matter what exposure plants are given, they should be turned occasionally to keep their growth erect. Plants have a natural tendency to lean toward the light. This is especially noticeable in seedlings that grow rapidly.

Some plants respond to the number of hours of light available in a day. This phenomenon is called photoperiodism and is important for growing special plants, such as poinsettias or greenhouse *Chrysanthemums.* Both of these plants are what is called short-day plants. Their flower buds will set (begin to develop) only when the days are short, about eight to ten hours of light per day. (Commercial 'mum growers shade their plants with black cloth to shorten the day.) Long-day plants are those which set flowers normally in a twelve- to sixteen-hour day.

To put this phenomenon to practical use with poinsettias, plants that have been kept from a previous Christmas should be tended carefully in the fall to assure Christmas flowers. From October 1 until the end of November, poinsettias require a short day. From 5:00 P.M. to 8:00 A.M. the next morning the plant should be kept in a room that is absolutely dark. Even a brief moment of a light turned on in a room is enough to break the cycle and delay flowering. If no room is available for constant darkness from 5:00 P.M. to 8:00 A.M., put the poinsettia in a large closet, but be sure to take it out every morning and care for it with proper watering when needed.

Hanging spider plants and episcias attached to an inside brick apartment wall provide a corner of greenery, adding to the window sill collection.

water

Home gardeners often seem to feel that they have to do something special for their plants. So they water them and water them, often killing them in the process. Actually, plants grow best with minimum attention.

The first and most important rule when watering any plant is: *water it thoroughly*. The most frequent complaint of people who say they have brown thumbs is, "But I do water my plants regularly, and they just die." The question is, how much water? A few tablespoonfuls every day are not going to do the plant much good. They only wet the top layer of soil. Meanwhile, the roots in the dry soil at the bottom of the pot shrivel and die. Thorough watering means to saturate the soil—from top to bottom.

How to tell when the soil is saturated? There is only one way: when the excess water seeps out through the drainage hole at the bottom. Make a mental note of how much water is needed to soak the soil, and give the plant this much water each time.

How often should plants be watered? For most plants, the soil should be allowed to dry out to some degree between waterings. This enables air to get to the roots, which need oxygen. Also, it keeps the plant in a state of gradual growth so that it maintains itself at a minimum level. The soil will have a dry look when it is ready for water, and the thirsty plant will have a rather languid look, almost as if it were going to wilt.

Since light, heat, ventilation, and other conditions affecting plants are never constant in homes, no set rule can be laid down about how often to water—whether it should be every day, once a week, or something in between. The frequency depends on the plant's performance.

The old arguments over whether to water from the top or from the bottom (by using a saucer) are not heard much these days. They must have been started by people who were rotting the crowns of their African violets and strawberry geraniums by overwatering. If watering is done carefully, however, all plants can be watered directly on the soil. This can be done easily with a long-spout watering can. A bulb-type baster, of the type used in the kitchen for basting roasts, is good, too, for small plants. It's easier to control. One reason for being finicky about watering African violets is that their leaves spot if cold water is dropped on them.

Watering plants in large tubs that have no drainage holes can be a bit of a puzzlement, for it is difficult to tell if the soil is soaked through. But agricultural research scientists have devised a method that works very well. Insert a funnel into the top of the soil. Pour water into the funnel, keeping track of the amount used, until no

A long-spout watering can makes it possible to water easily without spilling.

more water disappears. Soil will take up only as much water as it can absorb. When it absorbs no more, it is saturated. Remove the funnel by poking a finger into the soil to seal off the funnel's bottom opening. Remember how much water was poured into the funnel, and pour this amount directly on the soil every time the tubbed plant is watered.

Some large indoor trees, such as *Dracaena,* can thrive very well if they are watered as seldom as twice a month. But most plants require more frequent watering. The best schedule must be worked out for each plant.

One final tip on watering: room-temperature water is always better than cold tap water. So mix in a little warm water when filling the watering can.

air, temperature, and humidity

The quality of the air around plants greatly influences their rate of growth. This has been proved in controlled-environment experiments by plant scientists. When plants have been grown in greenhouses where air and other conditions are ideal, their growth has exceeded all expectations. In contrast, scientists are finding that air pollutants, such as ozone, sulfur dioxide, and fluorides, have detrimental effects not only on outdoor trees, shrubs, and garden plants, but also on plants growing in greenhouses that have no environmental controls.

A good air supply is basic to plant growth. It is an important ingredient of that still mystifying phenomenon, photosynthesis, whereby the leaves take in carbon dioxide from the air, convert it to carbohydrates, and release oxygen.

Fresh air is good for all plants, and frequent airing of a room where plants are growing is always sensible. But be cautious about opening windows directly in front of plants. No plant should be in a draft. Some plants, such as poinsettias, will drop leaves if exposed to drafts. If

Calamondin orange and azalea thrive in cool temperatures.

plants are in a bedroom near a window that is opened at night, move them away from the window so they will be out of the draft. This is especially important in winter. Also, if plants are growing on windowsills, be sure that the windows are sealed properly. Drafts of cold air seeping in can retard growth.

In an increasing number of homes, air conditioning is an influence on plant growth. Although the device nicely filters and cools the air, it also makes the air less humid, and plant growers need to provide more humidity (see page 21).

Plants should not be placed near fans, which cause rapid loss of moisture from the leaves. This lost water has to be replaced quickly by the roots, and a constant, rapid cycle like this has harmful effects. The plant appears to be "drying up." The important point to remember about the quality of air around plants is: nothing in excess.

Since the temperature in most homes and apartments is kept between 68 and 72 degrees for human comfort, plants well adapted to this range of temperature are the easiest to grow. Thanks to house-plant hunters and propagators, there are a vast number of such plants. A temperature drop of a few degrees at night also suits most plants.

There are cool-climate plants, of course, that do not thrive at normal house temperatures. Among them are *Camellia*, azaleas, some orchids, *Cyclamen*, and hardy bulbs that are being forced to flower. Fortunately, most of these plants are for seasonal display and can be bought already in bloom from commercial growers. Because of the contrast between a cool greenhouse and a warm home, the life-span of these gift plants is likely to be short. Obviously such plants will last longer if kept at least part of the time in a cool place.

Two other points should be made about temperature. If plants are kept near a window in winter, check the temperature there. During cold weather, the temperature near single-paned windows can be as much as 10 degrees lower than that of the rest of the room. Double paning usually avoids this. Some people tack up a clear sheet of polyethylene around the inside frame of a single-paned window, but this can cause condensation. If the temperature near a window gets too cold, the best course is to move plants away until the weather becomes warmer.

The second point is never to place plants near radiators or heating units. The higher temperature makes plants lose water faster through their leaf surfaces, drying them out. It is all right, however, to keep plants on top of a thick wood or asbestos shelf placed on a radiator. The shelf insulates the plants from the heat. The little bottom warmth that they receive is often beneficial, especially for African violets and flame violets, but no plants should ever be placed directly over heat.

A few plants are quite precise in their temperature requirements for bloom. Recent laboratory work on the influence of temperature on flower-bud set has shown this. Gardenias are now known to require a night temperature below 65 degrees to ensure setting of flower buds. But once the buds have set, the night tempera-

A tray filled with pebbles that are kept constantly wet is one of the best ways to provide humidity for indoor plants.

ture should not go below 70 degrees. In like manner, Christmas cactus requires a cool spell in the fall to trigger flower-bud set for holiday bloom. Keep these plants at temperatures below 68 degrees, but above 42 degrees, in early fall for a few weeks, then grow them in normal temperatures.

Moisture in the air is vital to the growth of most popular house plants because they come from tropical regions where there is superabundant rainfall. Obviously, this "wet" rain-forest atmosphere is beyond reason for the home, where the average humidity level is only about 40 to 50 percent.

Nevertheless, there are ways to provide higher humidity for plants. The easiest way is to group plants together on a tray filled with pebbles that are kept wet. The bottoms of the pots should rest on the pebbles and the water level kept *below* the tops of the pebbles. Otherwise, the plant soil would be soggy and the plants would have constant "wet feet." The gradual evaporation of the water into the air provides higher humidity. This setup is not a substitute for regular watering. Plants grouped together also benefit one another by giving off moisture into the air from their leaves in the natural process of transpiration.

Metal or plastic trays for pebbles are available in a limited selection of sizes and shapes in garden centers. Or metal trays can be made to size for window shelves, room dividers, or elsewhere by sheet-metal specialists. Large floor trays permit interesting plant arrangements to be made in living rooms or dining areas. Stones or gravel for these trays are sold by greenhouse suppliers, builders' suppliers, and pet shops.

Another way to provide humidity is to mist plants daily with a sprayer. For some plants, such as orchids, this is a necessity. The numerous sprayers on the market hold anywhere from a pint to a quart of water. If misting can be done without damaging walls, rugs, or draperies, it is an excellent humidifier. For large indoor garden areas, there are electric humidifiers—either utilitarian types or decorative fountains.

Of course, plants can be grown in the bathroom or the kitchen, where the natural humidity is high, providing there is sufficient light.

soil

S oil of the right quality is vital to greenery. Plants from a greenhouse or other commercial grower usually are in proper soil. But when these plants need repotting, or when seedlings are to be started, or when a planter is to be filled, thoughts turn to soil and the many recipes for potting mixtures.

Soil used for house plants is far from just plain dirt. It is made up of many ingredients, the three main parts being sand, clay, and humus. Sand, which consists of rock particles, makes soil porous so that water drains easily through it. Clay consists of very fine, powdery grains that pack hard and glue themselves together when wet. Clay helps hold soil together, giving it solidity. Humus is an assortment of organic matter in various stages of decay—leaves, stems, roots, and animal matter. The humus content supplies many nutrients necessary for plant growth and adds greatly to the soil's ability to retain moisture.

The favorite potting-soil recipe for general house-plant needs is equal parts of builders'

23

sand, garden soil high in clay content, and humus (generally sold in the form of rotted compost or peat moss). This basic mixture drains well, allows air to reach a plant's roots, and provides proper nutrients. It is excellent for all common house plants, and the home gardener will seldom go wrong using it. Many people who have a large number of plants mix soil in quantity and store it in their garage or shed.

A person who lives in a city or who has just a few plants in the home may prefer to buy his soil from the local garden center or dime store. Premixed soils in neat polyethylene bags are available for different plants, such as cacti, *Philodendron,* and African violet. There are also packages of separate ingredients for home blending. Packaged mixes and mixing ingredients have been sterilized, which eliminates fungus diseases that often fell seedlings or young plants raised from cuttings.

Those who mix their own soil from ingredients they have gathered themselves should sterilize it. The old-fashioned way was to bake the soil in the oven for about an hour at a low temperature. But the odor of baking soil is not a pleasant one to subject the family to. Chemical sterilization is much simpler. The chemicals are poisonous, however, so be extra cautious if there are little children and pets about.

Soil is sterilized with commercial formalin (40 percent formaldehyde). For one bushel of soil, mix two and one-half tablespoons of formalin in a cup of water. Sprinkle the solution over the soil, mix it in thoroughly, and keep the soil covered in an out-of-the-way place for twenty-four hours. Then uncover the soil and air it for several days. All odor should be gone

Pre-mix soil before starting repotting of plants.

24

CORNELL PEATLITE MIXES (one bushel volume)

	mix A	foliage plant mix	epiphytic mix
sphagnum peat moss	1/2 bushel	1/2 bushel	1/3 bushel
vermiculite (#2-3-4-size)	1/2 bushel	1/4 bushel	—
perlite (medium grade)	—	1/4 bushel	1/3 bushel
Douglas fir bark (1/8–1/4")	—	—	1/3 bushel
ground dolomitic limestone	5 Tbs.	8 Tbs.	8 Tbs.
20 percent superphosphate	2 Tbs.	2 Tbs.	6 Tbs.
10–10–10 fertilizer	3 Tbs.	3 Tbs.	3 Tbs.
potassium or calcium nitrate	—	1 Tbs.	1 Tbs.
granular wetting agent or	3 Tbs.	3 Tbs.	3 Tbs.
liquid wetting agent	1 tsp.	1 tsp.	1 tsp.
soluble trace element mix	see below*		

*Trace elements are needed in extremely small quantities. Overapplication can result in severe plant injury. Prepare a stock solution by dissolving one ounce of Soluble Trace Element Mix in one quart of water. Use 1/3 cup of stock solution added to a sufficient volume of water (one gallon) to get good distribution in one bushel of mix. Do not add more than this amount. Do not repeat the application. (For sources of ingredients, see page 255.)

before the soil is used.

As people take up the challenges of growing many kinds of plants, they often vary soil recipes a bit to suit their own needs and fancies. For instance, cacti may thrive better with a higher sand content in the soil. The waxplant, too, needs earth that is a bit more gritty. Some tropical plants grow better with more humus in the soil. Interesting results can be achieved by experimenting.

Gaining rapidly in popularity are the sterile, soil-less mixes developed by agricultural colleges. These mixes are light in weight, which facilitates the shipping of plants from greenhouse to retailer. Soil-less mixes are often used for growing plants under fluorescent light because the mixes are easy to handle and are especially suited for plants that flourish in this light.

One of the best known of these mixes is the Cornell Peatlite Mix developed by James W. Boodley and Raymond Sheldrake, Jr. The general-purpose mix and two variations are given on the facing page.

mix A Recommended for general garden plants, for starting vegetable seedlings, and for flowers.

foliage-plant mix Recommended for those plants which need growing media with high moisture-retention characteristics. Plants having a fine root system or possessing many fine root hairs are included in this group.

Amaryllis	Caladium
Aphelandra	Cissus
Begonia	Citrus
Beloperone	Coleus
Buxus	Ferns

Ficus   Palms
Hedera   Pilea
Helxine   Sansevieria
Maranta   Tolmiea
Oxalis

epiphytic mix   Recommended for plants which
require good drainage and aeration and have
the ability to withstand drying between waterings. Plants having coarse, tuberous, or rhizomatous roots are in this category.

African violets   Gloxinias
Aglaonema   Hoya
Aloe   Monstera
Bromeliads   Nephthytis
Cacti   Peperomia
Crassula   Philodendron
Dieffenbachia   Pothos
Episcia   Syngonium
Geraniums

fertilizer

W ater in the soil dissolves nutrients in the soil and these nutrients are then absorbed with the water by a plant's roots. Soil nutrients, which are necessary for plant growth, come from many sources: decaying plant and animal matter, air, water, and the rock minerals that broke down eons ago and made soil. When nutrients are plentiful, plants flourish. Eventually, many of the nutrients in the soil are absorbed by actively growing plants, and the supply must be replenished. This is done by adding fertilizer to the soil. Fertilizers also must be applied regularly to most of the packaged soil-less mixes which have no nutrients.

Sometimes you hear a plant described as a heavy feeder. This is a plant that requires a large supply of nutrients because of its rapid growth rate. A common example is the Kafir lily. Without plenty of nutrients, this plant never does well.

Most house plants are not heavy feeders. They absorb a small amount of nutrients over a long period of time. Overfeeding this type of plant does more harm than good. If nutrients are not absorbed readily by the plant roots, they accumulate in the soil, causing a toxic buildup. Eventually, roots can be burned. Excess fertilizer salts seep through porous clay pots and form deposits on the exteriors. Or they form crusts around the rims of plastic pots. Often, fertilizer crusts build up on the surface of the soil.

Excess buildup of chemical fertilizer salts should make it clear that it is unwise to feed and feed plants that are in poor states of vigor. Plants do not require "vitamins," and an extra dose of fertilizer is not going to boost them into health.

The three main nutrients needed by plants are nitrogen, phosphorus, and potassium. Fertilizers contain varying amounts of these nutrients, the potassium being present in the form of one of its compounds, potash. The percentage of each nutrient contained in a fertilizer is given on the package in the form of three numbers, such as 5–10–5, 20–20–20, or 10–20–15. The first number represents the percentage of nitrogen (N), the second phosphorus (P), and the third potash (K). In addition to the big three, small amounts of many trace elements are included in the fertilizer formula, but these are not expressed in the ratio numbers. The trace elements include boron, calcium, copper, iron, manganese, molybdenum, sulphur, and zinc.

Nitrogen is the most quickly absorbed nutrient. It gives the leaves a rich green color. Phosphorus develops strong stems and good root systems. Potassium encourages the development of flower buds and strong growth.

For indoor plants, the best fertilizers are water-soluble, high-analysis types. Water-soluble fertilizers dissolve immediately in water and are ready to be taken up by the roots without delay. Results are visible in a few days. High-analysis fertilizers can be recognized by the high numbers in the ratios, such as 20–20–20, 30–10–10, or 20–5–10.

Choice of a fertilizer ratio should be guided by what a plant seems to need. For example, when flower buds are setting, high potassium will encourage strong buds; if foliage is yellow, high nitrogen is indicated. Some fertilizers are from chemical sources, others from organic sources, especially fish emulsions. But regardless of source, there is little difference in the quality of the nutrients.

Fertilizers are sold under a variety of trade names, all having different formulations and dilution directions. The labels must be read carefully and the directions followed to be sure of using the product correctly. A source list is provided in the Appendix.

The standard granular fertilizers used for lawns and gardens are not as practical for house plants because they do not dissolve quickly in water. Their chemicals must break down first into simpler compounds before they dissolve and are available for root absorption. These granular formulations are best used when large quantities of potting soil are being mixed. They can be blended thoroughly with sand, humus, and loam.

When should you give a plant fertilizer? No one rule is suitable except for plants that are raised under artificial light. These plants are exposed to a constant amount of light daily. They have no cloudy days or dormant seasons. Therefore they can be given applications of fertilizer at regular intervals, usually once a week. About once every four to six weeks, however, they should be given clear water, instead of water containing dissolved fertilizer, to flush out any buildup of fertilizer salts.

Plants growing in natural light need fertilizer less frequently. One rule of thumb is to apply fertilizer whenever a plant grows a new leaf. Directions on fertilizer packages often say to fertilize plants every ten days or two weeks. This sells a lot of fertilizer. But each plant and each set of growing conditions requires a different rate of fertilization, so each person must be his own judge.

In spring, summer, and fall, when there is plenty of sunlight, plants grow actively and need more fertilizer than in winter, when many go into a semidormant state. Some plants, especially flowering types, require frequent applications of plant nutrients when the buds are setting and just before the flowers bloom. Large foliage plants—*Philodendron, Dracaena,* Swiss cheese plant—grow slowly and may need fertilizer only two or three times a year. When too many leaves start to yellow, the plant may need fertilizer.

Acid-type fertilizer is now available in small quantities for those plants that grow best in an acid soil. Gardenia is the best known of the acid-soil plants. *Camellia* and azaleas also require acid-type fertilizer.

potting and pruning

I ndoor plants are usually kept in pots made of clay or plastic. Clay pots were the first type made for indoor plants. They are the best known and generally the best liked. Their advantages are good drainage and porosity. Excess moisture in the soil seeps out through the drainage hole in the bottom of the pot and through the porous sides. The hole and porous sides also permit air to reach the plant's roots. Many people like the natural color of clay pots. Their big disadvantage is that they are heavy, especially when the soil inside them is wet. Also, they crack and break easily.

Plastic pots are a more recent innovation. Their chief merit is their light weight, and some people prefer their decorative colors. Plastic pots have holes in the bottom for drainage, but the pots are not porous, so neither water nor air passes through their sides. As a result, plants growing in them do not require as much water. This is important because many people tend to overwater plants growing in plastic pots, and roots often rot. Few people realize that the roots are decaying until the plant begins to turn yellow and eventually dies.

Although "pot" is the general term used for plant containers, there are also pans. Pans are wider than they are tall and are most often used as containers for hardy bulbs that are to be forced to bloom early, and for gift plants, chiefly *Azalea*. Pots, on the other hand, are taller than they are wide. Pot sizes are indicated by inches which measure the diameter across the top. Sizes range from two to more than twelve inches. Saucers are usually available to fit the various size pots.

The "see-through" pots are made of heavy-grade clear plastic. As roots grow around and around in the pot, many of them are exposed to view. As far as can be determined, the exposure of the roots to light does not limit plant growth as the roots are enclosed and protected from air which would dry them out. Again, as with all plastic pots, be cautious about overwatering. The plastic does not breathe as does clay and moisture is retained for longer periods.

To pot a plant in a clay or plastic pot, first see that the container is clean and that the soil is on hand, ready to use. In the bottom of a clay pot place a shard or piece of broken pot or a few stones over the drainage hole. This stops the soil from running out the bottom. Plastic pots have several smaller holes, which need not be covered.

Now put a handful of soil in the pot, pouring it in freely without packing it down. Next, with the stem of the plant held between thumb and forefinger and the roots extending down into the pot, put soil around the roots with the other hand, keeping the stem erect. Pour soil in until

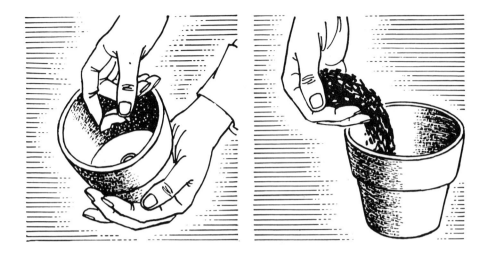

To pot a plant, place a piece of crock over the drainage hole
to prevent the soil from running out, then pour a little soil
into the bottom of the pot.

Set the plant into the pot so that its roots will be well covered.
Pour soil around the roots until the pot is filled to the top.
Then press the soil down firmly with your thumbs, and water.

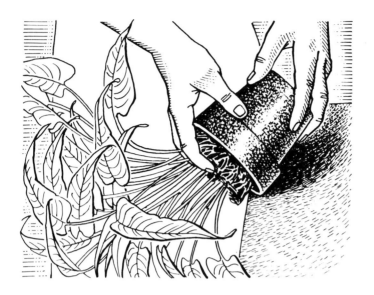

To determine if a pot is rootbound, turn the pot upside down and knock it against the side of a table while supporting the open end with the other hand.

A mass of roots twining around the soil indicates that it is time to shift the plant to a pot one size larger.

it reaches the rim of the pot. Then press the soil firm with the thumbs, moving them around the inside rim of the pot. This should be all the "tucking in" that the plant needs. Some old pros like to pick up the pot and bang it on the table just to be sure all the roots are in contact with the soil.

Water the plant thoroughly. The watering will settle the soil and remove any air pockets.

After a time a plant will outgrow its pot and need to be shifted to a larger pot. There are several ways to know if a plant needs repotting. The most obvious is to turn the pot upside down and, using one hand to support the plant, knock the rim of the pot on the end of a table or bench. If the plant has a compact root ball, it will slip out easily. A network of roots twining around the soil indicates a need for repotting. Another way to tell if a plant is "pot-bound" is to see if the roots have pushed out through the drainage hole. Or, if a plant has many yellow leaves and hasn't grown much lately, it may need repotting.

There is one basic rule for repotting: shift the plant to a pot that is only one size larger than the one the plant was in. In other words, a plant in a four-inch pot should be transplanted to a five-inch pot. There is a good reason for this. If the roots are put in too large a pot, they will have such a busy time spreading and growing that leaf and top growth will be sacrificed. Most plants are at their best if their roots are just a tiny bit crowded.

When repotting, use a fresh soil mix and follow the directions for potting, as described earlier. If the root ball of the plant is very tightly packed and hard, it can be squeezed a bit to break it apart. Some of the thicker root pieces can be cut if needed.

Trees in tubs can be maintained for many years without shifting by merely changing the top layer of the soil. Scrape several inches of soil off the top, but be careful not to damage any surface roots. Then replace this old soil with freshly mixed soil, and water it well.

When decorative jardinieres, ceramic bowls, antique urns, or tubs are used as plant containers, pots are usually fitted inside them. But if this is impossible and a plant has to be set directly in a container with no drainage holes, the planting must be done carefully. At the bottom of the container, place a layer of shards, gravel, stones, or any similar material that will provide a space into which excess water can drain. This drainage layer should be three inches deep, more or less, depending on the size of the container. The soil mixture should be gritty so that it will not pack down but remain friable and drain well. Sand imparts this quality to soil, as do inorganic materials such as perlite and vermiculite.

Plants growing in containers without drainage have to be watered carefully. After a few weeks of experience with these plants, a wise judgment can be made on exactly how much water is needed to keep the plant soil properly moist. The funnel system described in the watering section is an excellent means of learning how much water is required to wet the soil through.

Pruning is for training and shaping a plant. Almost every house plant can stand a bit of this from time to time. The only exceptions are African violet, strawberry geranium, and other plants that grow from crowns—that is, from growing points near the soil. This type of growth is not pruned. Of course, the best time to prune any plant is when it is young. Training a plant by pruning it a few times *before* it matures is much better than cutting it back severely *after* it matures. But even a mature plant, such as a geranium, comes back substantially if it is pruned back sharply to make it more shapely and attractive.

Woody plants such as gardenia, *Citrus,* and *Fuchsia* should be shaped with small shrub-pruning shears. Gardenia, for example, grows "suckers" from the lower part of the plant's stem. These young shoots should be cut off to keep the plant growing decoratively. *Fuchsia* often sends out wild wisps that should be cut back to conform to the overall shape of the plant.

Soft-stemmed plants such as *Coleus* and *Philodendron* can be pruned by pinching the stems between thumbnail and forefinger. Always prune immediately above a node—the growing point where a leaf is attached. Cuts made here usually force branching below the cut, except in the case of mature succulent plants whose stems have become woody.

When plants grow too tall—to the ceiling, for example—air layering (see page 245) is a means of getting them under control and at the same time gaining an extra plant.

tender
loving care

An important part of house plant care is removing faded blossoms and yellowed leaves promptly, especially on oxalis.

Good housekeeping is just a matter of tidiness as far as indoor plants are concerned. Nothing mars a handsome plant collection more quickly than yellowed leaves, soiled pots, faded flowers, or spotted foliage. Although it is difficult to check a large collection of plants constantly, try to form the habit of removing any yellowed foliage or marred leaves whenever you see them. Plan to give an hour or more a week to a large collection for general housekeeping and tidying up.

Foliage plants always become dusty, especially in large cities or in areas near heavy industries. One of the simplest ways to keep large leaves clean is to wash them off about once a month with a soft sponge and a bucket of warm water. For very dusty, sticky leaves, mild soapsuds will help, but be sure to rinse them off afterward. Avoid using milky or waxy substances that make the leaves shine, for these clog the stomata, the leaf's breathing pores.

Foliage of smaller plants is easier to clean by taking the plants to the kitchen sink and rinsing

To keep smooth leaved plants such as this ti plant clean, wipe them with moistened cotton.

40

the leaves under the faucet once a week. Frequent misting with a hand sprayer will also help to keep leaves clean. This is best for fuzzy-leaved plants such as African violets.

Don't forget the pots, tubs, jardinieres, or planters that the plants are growing in. When fertilizer salts or mold accumulates on the outside of clay pots or around the rims of plastic pots, scrub it off with a stiff brush and warm water. If fertilizer crust appears on the surface of the soil, scrape off the top layer of soil and replace it with fresh soil. Tubs and jardinieres become grimy. Wash them once in a while. Planters, especially wooden types, become dull and can be waxed and polished a few times a year to improve their appearance.

A vacation outdoors in the summer benefits most house plants. Those that normally thrive in the sunshine—geraniums, *Citrus,* and Kafir lily, for instance—can be put in sunny sites. If there are just a few plants, select a strategic place in the flower border and sink the pots into the ground to their rims. To prevent a plant's roots from working out of the pot holes and anchoring in the ground, put a thick layer of shards, gravel, or ashes in the bottom of the hole before sinking the pots. The house plants will have to be watered more frequently than the garden plants since their roots are confined inside the pot and do not have direct access to natural ground moisture.

Gardenias, large *Philodendron,* umbrella trees, *Dracaena,* and other tropical or foliage plants should be placed in a semishaded location outdoors. Underneath an open-branched tree or a lath-roofed patio, they will get filtered sun. These large plants will need careful attention during long hot spells to be sure they are kept moist. Soft-leaved plants such as African violets are best left indoors or put on a screened patio or porch. Strong summer sun is not for them.

Before the vacationing plants are brought indoors to join the others, they should be given careful inspection and pruning back. Inspection is for insect pests, especially spiders, aphids, white fly or any other "unwanteds." If found, sometimes a good showering with the hose is enough to knock them off. Check in a few days; if they are still there, apply a household aerosol containing pyrethrins or malathion.

Pruning back is usually necessary as plants thrive outdoors and expand greatly in size. Prune them hard with a sharp knife to give them a compact shape. Save the prunings and root them for cuttings.

Bring plants that are vacationing outside back into the home around Labor Day weekend so they can adjust to the environment before the heat is turned on.

Vacationers need not call in a plant sitter for plants that have to stay in the house. A large plastic bag will do. One from the cleaner's is ideal to make a "holding greenhouse." The day before going on vacation, water all plants carefully. Check to be sure they are free of insect pests; otherwise the closed environment within the plastic bag will provide an ideal chamber for their increase! Keep all similar plant types together in separate bags—fuzzy leafed plants such as African violets and smooth-foliage plants such as *Dracaena* and *Philodendron*.

Southern yew, African violet, Ivy and a host of others will "keep" while you are on vacation if they are watered and covered with a plastic bag, fastened with a rubber band.

Place the opened bag on a kitchen table or cupboard located in good light but not direct sun. Slide the plants upright into the wide opened end of the bag, keeping enough space between plants so the leaves do not touch. Use as many bags as necessary. When they are filled, place a rubber band over the ends of each bag to keep them airtight. Enjoy your vacation. Plants will keep this way for at least two months. The important thing is to water each plant thoroughly first and be sure the table or cupboard is in a light, not sunny, location. (Sunlight will cause too rapid growth, increase leaf transpiration, and raise temperatures inside the plastic "greenhouse.") Also, the bags must not have perforations or tears. For a very large indoor plant, place a large-sized cleaner bag over the plant and fasten the open end around the rim of the pot.

For a short vacation—five days to a week— water plants thoroughly and place away from sunlight and they should keep.

*Poor light and worn out
soil produced leggy
weak growth on this
shrimp plant.*

trouble
signs

W hen plants do not thrive as well as they should, they often show visible clues as to what is ailing them. Once the plant's trouble is known, it usually can be corrected.

Novice house-plant growers, however, are often overzealous in looking for such troubles and trying to correct them. As soon as a leaf yellows or develops a brown spot, they run for a remedy. Frequently their solution is a generous dash of fertilizer—just about the worst approach. Or they may squirt the plant with a household pesticide. Not much better!

In the majority of cases, the plant's problem is none other than a simple cultural fault. Here are some of the most common symptoms of poor culture. All can be corrected by changes in the growing methods.

*When soil becomes
compacted it should be
aerated with a fork.*

Physiological adjustment occurs when a plant raised in the nearly ideal conditions of a temperature-controlled greenhouse or cool, shaded

46

nursery field in a warmer section of the country is brought into a home. The plant suffers "shock," dropping a few usually older leaves as it adjusts to the new environment. This is particularly true of gift plants sold for the holiday seasons. When this occurs, pull off the yellowed leaves and continue normal care, watering the plant regularly as needed. If leaf yellowing continues for a longer period than seems reasonable, move the plant to a place where the lighting is different and change the watering schedule. Refer also to the directions given for individual plant care in the "Plants to Grow" section.

Overwatering fills the porous spaces of the soil with water instead of air and thus prevents a plant's roots from getting the oxygen they need for proper growth. This lack of oxygen, usually accompanied by a leaching of soil nutrients, often damages roots and endangers the plant. Yellow leaves are signals.

To remedy oversoaked soil, withhold water until the plant almost wilts. Then gradually begin a new watering program. After a week or two, apply a water-soluble house-plant fertilizer. If the plant is still doing poorly, repot it in fresh soil.

Hunger, or lack of nutrients, is indicated by a gradual yellowing of leaves. The yellowing usually begins at the outer edges of a leaf and then spreads to the whole leaf. Sometimes the soil simply needs fertilizer, but more often the nutrient shortage is the result of the plant having outgrown its pot (see page 33). The roots need more soil from which to get nutrients. Applying fertilizer is a quick remedy for a pot-bound plant, but the longer-term remedy is to repot by shifting the plant to a pot one size larger than the one in which it is growing.

Small leaves are a complaint most often heard from those who are growing *Philodendron*. As new leaves appear, they are smaller and smaller. The reason is poor light. Try moving the plant to a brighter location. Keep the leaves free of dust, too, by rinsing them off frequently in a sink, using room-temperature water. This will also give the plant periodic increases in humidity, another way to encourage larger leaves.

Although it sounds contradictory, too much light can also cause smaller leaves. This may occur with African violets that are in a bright, sunny, south window with no relief from the hot sun's rays. Try a new location for such plants.

Leaf spots on foliage plants are usually caused by too much sun. When these brown spots appear consistently, move the plant to a place where it gets less sunlight. Spattering the leaves of any plant with hot or very cold water droplets may also cause spotting. Hairy-leaved plants, such as African violet, are especially sensitive to cold-water droplets.

Brown-edged leaves are often the result of careless tending. Perhaps a plant is neglected and the soil is allowed to dry out frequently. Then the soil is flooded with water, damaging the plant's roots. Browning of leaf edges reflects this damage. Brown edges also occur when a plant near an open door or window is exposed to cold drafts. Another cause is the accumulation of fertilizer salt on the edges of pots. When leaves rest against this, they develop a brown edge. Scrub the edge of the pot and in the future remember to flush the soil with clear water

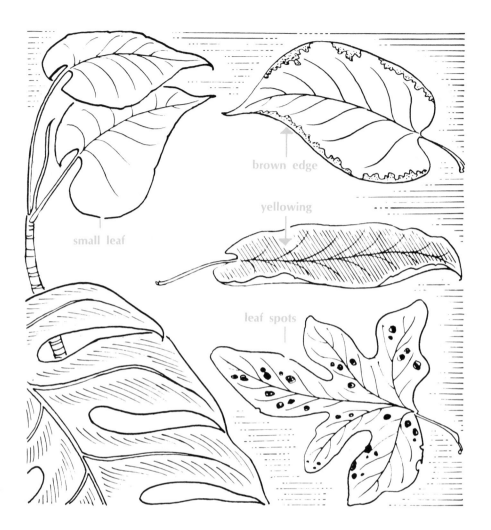

to prevent an accumulation of salts.

Leggy plants occur when stems become overly long because they are reaching for more light or because they are growing in a room that is too warm. Move such plants to a brighter and cooler location.

No flowers may be the result of overfeeding plants to induce lush foliage. Withhold fertilizer applications, especially during winter months. Sometimes an abrupt break in routine, such as a drying off of the soil for a short time or a change of light exposure, will cause a "lazy" plant to flower. Flower-booster fertilizers are recommended for plants that are not overfed.

No growth is usually a sign of insufficient light. The plant exists in a languid state, neither producing new leaves nor growing larger. Many plants are particularly sensitive to light shortages, including African violet, *Columnea*, cacti and succulents, flame violet, *Nautilocalyx*, and waxplant.

pests

W here do they come from, those creepers and crawlers that suddenly appear on house plants much to the dismay of the owners? Plant pests come from many sources. Often they come in on a new plant, undetected by the grower or buyer. Or another plant in a collection can be a source. A few insects may be in the soil used to pot plants or may fly in from outdoors.

The best way to prevent insects from colonizing plants is to give the plants good regular care. Frequent misting and washing of foliage, for example, helps keep pests away. A new plant should be isolated for several weeks before it is added to a major collection. If any insect pests are present, they will appear by this time and can be eliminated before the plant joins the others. Occasional close inspections of leaf axils, of the backs of leaves, of growing tips, and of areas around flower buds during routine tending may uncover pests.

When pests do appear, the plants affected should be isolated immediately. Many pests can be controlled by taking plants to a sink where the foliage can be washed under the faucet. Cover the soil in the pot with paper and one hand while turning the pot on its side so that foliage can be placed under the faucet. Washing foliage several times a week will often rid plants of light infestations of mealybugs, red spider mites, and white flies. For heavier infestations, spraying may be necessary. Sprays in aerosol cans clearly marked for use on house plants are easiest and safest for indoor use.

When using a house-plant aerosol, follow the label directions carefully. Indoors, a good plan is to spray in an isolated area, such as the basement, or in an apartment hallway. Spray the plant carefully, especially the undersides of the leaves. Allow it to drain or dry off for an hour or so, before bringing it back.

The insects most likely to be found on house plants are described below. Specific controls for them are included just in case the few simple methods already suggested don't do the job.

ants House plants infested with aphids, mealybugs, or scale often attract ants because these pests excrete a honeydew upon which ants feed. Control the other pests first, and the ants should disappear.

aphids These insects are green, black, or red with soft pear-shaped bodies and long legs. Some have wings; others are wingless. They accumulate on young succulent growing tips and flower buds, where they suck the plant juices and cause stunting as well as distorted buds and leaves. Some kinds feed on roots. Wash foliage to get rid of light infestations; use rotenone or

malathion spray for large populations.

earthworms Though gardeners quite rightly have a respect for earthworms, they have no place in pots. Their burrowing in and around roots may do more harm than good, and the value of their castings is minimal in the small confines of a pot. Earthworms sometimes crawl into pots through drainage holes when house plants are sunk in the garden outdoors during the summer. One way to discourage this is to put a layer of gravel under the pot before setting it in the ground. To check for the presence of earthworms before bringing a pot back indoors, knock the root ball out of the pot by striking the edge of the pot against a hard surface while supporting the soil with your hand. If worms are found, put the plant in fresh soil.

fungus gnats These gnats occasionally lay eggs on house-plant soil. The eggs hatch into tiny white maggots which feed on plant roots. The maggots are most prevalent in soil mixtures containing high quantities of humus, peat moss, or leaf mold. Drenching the soil with limewater (available from the druggist) will control them.

mealybugs These insects are covered with a white fuzz that make them look like specks of cotton. These slow-moving insects suck the juices of plants. As a result, new leaves and flowers develop poorly. Mealybugs excrete a honeydew that attracts ants. The pests have favorite feeding places: in leaf axils, on the undersides of leaves, along leaf veins, and inside the protective coverings of flower buds. Mealybugs are most often found on African violet, gardenia, piggyback plants, *Coleus,* waxplant, cactus, croton, and *Begonia.*

Mealybugs are difficult to control, but they can be conquered with persistence. As soon as a tiny white fuzzy speck is detected, wash it off. If several are found, dip a cotton swab in rubbing alcohol and wipe the insects off the plants. If this is done carefully every few days, it may be sufficient to control the pests.

For a heavy infestation, isolate the plant and dip it in a large bucket of malathion liquid. Mix this by putting two teaspoons of 57 percent emulsifiable concentrate in each gallon of water. Add one-half teaspoon of household detergent as a wetter. To dip the plant, invert the pot, covering it and the soil with paper to prevent the soil from falling out. Allow the plant to dry, away from the sun. This dip may need to be repeated in two weeks.

millipedes and centipedes These are hard-bodied, wormlike creatures with many tiny legs. They feed on roots, tubers, bulbs, and underground stems. More a nuisance than a serious pest, they are unlikely to appear if plant areas are kept clean and free of decaying leaves, stems, and debris, in which they breed and hide.

red spider mites When large numbers of them are present, their webs make a plant's foliage appear dusty. They suck the plant's juices, and their attack causes leaves to become yellow or bronze, and then to fall. Unless controlled, red spider mites can destroy plants. The best control is prevention. Frequent syringing of plants keeps the foliage clean and dust-free. Be sure to rinse the undersides of leaves. A serious infestation of red spider mites can be stopped by dipping the plant in malathion, as described under *Mealybugs*. Very badly infested plants should be discarded to prevent them from spreading the mites to other plants. Ivy is a favorite diet of red spiders. New plants brought into the home should be immunized promptly. Badly infested plants can be treated the same way. Make a sinkful of lukewarm sudsy water using mild soap flakes. Swish the ivy stems through it with your hand for several minutes, then rinse thoroughly in clear lukewarm water. This should destroy any red spider present. Repeat if necessary in ten days. These mites thrive in a dry, warm, sunny environment and they can develop rapidly.

scale insects These white, brown, or black creatures are protected by a hard, rounded covering. Often they will go undetected for quite some time since they barely move and adhere to the backs of leaves, usually along the veins. Like mealybugs, to which they are related, scale insects suck plant juices. As a result, they stunt plant growth. They are most often found on ferns, palms, and cacti. For light infestations, use an old toothbrush to scrub the insects off the backs of leaves and stems. For serious cases, use malathion, as described under *Mealybugs*.

sowbugs and pillbugs These insects are oval-shaped and hard-bodied, about a quarter of an inch long. More a nuisance than a pest, they are active at night, feeding on decaying organic matter and sometimes on tender roots. They can be eradicated with malathion, as described under *Mealybugs*.

springtails These insects got their curious name from a curious tail-like appendage by which they spring away when disturbed. Small (one-quarter inch) white creatures, they feed on decaying organic matter and are most often found near ground level. Mainly a harmless nuisance, they can be controlled with a house-plant aerosol spray if their number becomes bothersome.

thrips Tiny, thin creatures, these are hard to see unless disturbed. Then they run rapidly or fly away. They feed on leaves and flowers by sucking out the plant juices. Damage appears as streaked areas with little black dots of excrement. House-plant aerosols or a malathion dip (see *Mealybugs*) will control them.

whiteflies These insects multiply very rapidly in a short period of time. When a plant that they have invaded is disturbed, these tiny flies whisk off in "clouds." They suck plant juices and cause leaves to turn yellow and eventually drop off. Sticky honeydew caused by their feeding attracts ants. To get rid of whiteflies, use a malathion or rotenone spray. Repeat weekly until the insects disappear. Greenhouse gardeners have often been successful in checking whitefly by hanging one or two Vapona strips in the house. This might be tried for a large indoor house-plant collection. But the strips should not be used near a kitchen, child's nursery, or dining room. They are available in hardware stores, supermarkets, discount stores, etc.

58

calendar
of
care

january

Pots of tulips, daffodils, crocus, and Dutch iris will be well rooted now. Choose one or two pots and start forcing the bulbs indoors. The pots should be brought into warm room temperatures gradually until leaves are beginning to develop, then into bright light and full sun as flower buds start to form.

Watch for white fly on fuchsia, lantana, and other plants. Isolate plants that are badly infested.

Geraniums stay verdant and green in the winter months if kept on the dry side and not overwatered. Feed only occasionally—about every four weeks (three weeks if blooming).

Pot amaryllis bulbs in a 6-inch pot.

Remember that gardenias like a cool, moist atmosphere to thrive. Mist them daily with room-temperature water.

february

Bring indoors a few more pots of rooted, hardy bulbs for forcing.

Sow seed of coleus, geraniums, cacti, and African violets.

Bring in some branches of forsythia and quince from the garden to force for bouquets.

Mist orchids daily to keep up their required humidity.

Pot new tubers of gloxinias, making sure to put them right side up; the rounded portion is the bottom.

Tuberous begonias planted now will be in bloom in time for Mother's Day gifts or in early bloom in window boxes.

If African violet bloom is languishing, the plants may need dividing and repotting. Separate bunched plant into individual pots and save a few sturdy leaves for cuttings.

march

Bring a few branches of lilac indoors to force into bloom.

This is a good month to air-layer indoor trees that are too tall, especially dracaenas, all figs, dieffenbachia, and schefflera.

Hanging planters will be surging into new growth as sunshine increases. Houseclean the planters now and check for any repotting or replacing that may be needed.

Check for mealybugs on coleus, piggyback plant, crotons, hoyas, and gardenias. Treatment may have to be repeated every ten days to destroy new hatching broods.

Start tubers of caladiums in a rich peaty mixture. Keep moist until new growth tips are well started.

Plant seed of the new hybrid geraniums or take cuttings of the scented geraniums.

Repot the camellia if it is needed and if blooms have faded.

april

There will be increasing sunlight from now on. Plants will respond well to more frequent feeding—every two to three weeks for active flowering species.

Move African violets and other light-sensitive plants away from strong sunlight to east or west windows.

Mist ferns often to maintain proper humidity for their growth.

Seedlings of plants sown earlier in the year will now be large enough to transplant to individual pots or to share with friends.

Cacti will start blooming now that there is more sunshine. Watering may be increased slightly.

This is a good time to take cuttings of gardenias which will develop during the summer for good-sized fall house plants.

Plant achimenes for summertime bloom.

may

Lantana and fuchsia seedlings are available at nurseries. Select a young, single-stemmed one and start training it for a standard. Geranium standards can be started now or in the fall.

In mild climates, after the Easter lily flowers fade, move the plant to the garden; it can be potted directly in the soil if there is a sunny, well-drained spot. The lily does not thrive outdoors where winters are severe.

Check again for invading pests which often fly in from the outdoors. Aphids may appear on succulent tips of seedlings. Isolate heavily infested plants.

Keep up with a regular fertilizing program for such heavy-feeding plants as gardenia, Kafir lily, begonias, and all in flower or buds. Foliage plants do not require as much fertilizer.

Turn pots of gloxinias every few days to keep leaves wide and flat-growing.

65

june

In cold climates, all danger of frost is past and the house plants may be moved outdoors for the summer. A partly shaded patio or area under large shade trees is ideal for the tropical foliage plants such as schefflera, figs, dracaenas, and the like. They should not be in direct sunlight. Flowering plants such as begonias, geraniums, lantanas, and fuchsias may be moved to sunnier areas or sunk into the ground in flower borders. Place a thick layer of gravel, ashes, or sand under the pots first before sinking them to their rims. This prevents the roots from growing through the drainage hole and anchoring in the soil.

Do not move soft-leaved plants such as gloxinias, African violets, and other gesneriads outdoors. They are better kept indoors or under a sheltered deck.

Clean up the indoor garden by dismantling: remove all pots, wash the drainage gravel, and allow the trays to dry out; disinfect and reassemble; clean all pots and check for pests or need to repot.

july

Plants that are sunk in the ground in flower borders should be turned every two to three weeks to be sure they are not rooting fast.

Do not forget to mist house plants indoors, as the humidity requirements are still needed. Be careful about placing plants near open windows where there are evening drafts.

If gloxinias are waning, start to dry off tubers and store them in their pots until early winter.

Orchids sometimes go through a summer slump. This is a good time to check plants for repotting. Use orchid fiber and be sure that pots are clean.

If going away on vacation, use the plastic bag greenhouse (Page 43) as the best means of care. Plants will thrive for weeks and often look better upon your return than they did when you left.

august

Take leaf cuttings of rex begonias and African violets.

Continue feeding lantanas and fuchsias being trained as standards. Rub off any side buds to keep the long "whip" growing.

Give pots sunk in the ground outdoors another turn so they do not root fast.

Order bulbs now for potting in fall for forcing: tulips, daffodils, crocus, hyacinths, and some of the little bulbs.

Sow seed of marigolds and nasturtiums indoors for fall bloom in sunny windows.

Pot oxalis bulbs for early fall flowers.

Save avocado pits for children to grow as their own special plants.

september

House plants should be moved indoors in colder climates before heat is turned on in the home. Before they are brought in, check carefully for pest infestation and "de-bug" where necessary. Cut back plants that have become wild and leggy and use the stems as cuttings for rooting. Repot any plants that have outgrown their original pots.

Take cuttings of border plants for house plants such as impatiens, geraniums, coleus, bloodleaf, and the like.

Gather from woodlands young seedlings and mosses for woodland terrariums. Do not pick any plants on conservation lists.

Hanging plants will be brought back indoors, too. Check them over for pests and trim back scraggly growth. Repotting should not be necessary.

Stock up on house plant supplies, especially pots, fertilizers, and soil ingredients.

october

To encourage bloom on poinsettias and Christmas cactus, follow light-control instructions, Pages 137 and 93.

Humidity will be important now that house heat will be on. Keep misters handy for hand misting and make use of pebble trays to keep moisture in the atmosphere.

Hardy bulbs are potted this month so they will form roots in time for forcing indoors in winter. Be sure there is a good, safe storage area for rooting, where the pots will be protected from freezing in severe winter climates; a garage, a deep coldframe, or a sod house is ideal.

Caladiums and tuberous begonias that were growing outdoors should now be dried off and allowed to go dormant. Store them in their pots or remove them from the pots and store them in slightly moistened peat or perlite. Tie individual varieties in separate plastic bags.

november

There will be decreasing sunlight for growth now. Do not overfeed plants.

Root cuttings of coleus, African violets, impatiens, begonias and the like for Christmas giving.

Check plants for mealybugs and white fly.

Remove plants from windowsills in cold climates where the early frosts cause quick temperature drops.

Pot African amaryllis and paperwhite narcissus for December bloom.

Sow seeds of begonias and African violets. Members of plant societies can exchange seeds of rare species which are often available during the winter months.

december

Pot rooted cuttings of gift plants early in the month so they will be ready for gift giving.

Keep poinsettia plants away from drafts.

Keep cyclamens cool and in a moist atmosphere.

Send a subscription to a garden magazine as a gift.

Apply for a gift membership to a plant society for a family friend or relative.

Keep holly and other cut greens for trimming in a cool place until they are arranged. Then mist them daily, if possible, to make them last longer.

Remember that there are many kinds of houseplant hobby accessories that can be given for gifts: pots, soil, seed packets, books, hand tools, misters, etc.

72

The most popular plants for indoor growing are discussed in the following pages and most of them are illustrated with watercolor drawings. Brief descriptions are given of the plants, their needs, and their care. Cultural recommendations can never be regimented into cut-and-dried growing instructions because each home has its own climate—temperature, humidity, and light. Variations in these conditions have different effects on individual plant growth. Therefore, the best any book can do is guide. Where particular needs of a plant are important, these have been pinpointed. Otherwise, the reader is advised to follow suggestions for average plant care, which are discussed in earlier pages and summarized here:

Soil consisting of equal parts of sand, garden soil, and humus is satisfactory for most plants.

Water plants thoroughly, then let soil dry out before watering again.

Humidity in the average home usually needs to be supplemented by frequent misting of plants or by keeping pots on a tray filled with moist pebbles.

Fertilizer should be applied to the soil of actively growing plants only when needed.

Light varies according to location in the home. A south window gets full sunlight, an east or west window moderate sun (in morning or afternoon), and a north window no sun. Curtains or screening are usually needed to filter strong summer sun.

Plants are arranged on the following pages in alphabetical order according to their common names. A name may refer to a single kind of plant, a group of similar plants, or a family of plant groups. Because variations in common names often cause confusion, the scientific name is given in parentheses after the common name. Different members of a plant group usually thrive under the same approximate growing conditions and care. Where specific differences occur, they are noted.

The most commonly grown house plants can be found on sale at garden centers, green-houses, dime stores, and some supermarkets. Choose those types of plants that will grow well under the conditions present in your home. When selecting an individual plant, examine it carefully to be sure that it is healthy and sturdy. Avoid plants with yellow leaves or other signs of trouble. Look at the backs of leaves and in leaf axils for insect pests. If any are found, choose another plant.

Unusual house plants are not likely to be found in neighborhood stores. They usually must be obtained by mail from nurseries and greenhouses that specialize in developing hybrids of house plants. The catalogs of such plant specialists are interesting to study. Some catalogs are free, some not.

Other sources of unusual indoor plants are the various house-plant societies. Many members of these societies raise unusual indoor plants and are often willing to exchange or sell them. Most such societies charge a nominal fee for annual membership dues. Many have their own publications, and a list is provided in the Appendix.

achimenes

Achimenes (*Achimenes*) are showy plants, many of which trail and can be grown in hanging baskets. Grow them in early spring from rhizomes (underground stems) potted in a light, humus-soil mixture and kept in an east or west window. When shoots are a few inches high, pinch them back to encourage branching. Small petunialike flowers—white, pink, yellow, blue, or violet—appear in summer. Keep soil moist; dryness discourages flowering. After flowers begin to fade, allow soil to become dry, for rhizomes are dormant from late fall to spring.   *Natural habitat:* Central American tropical regions.

African violets *(Saintpaulia ionantha)* bloom all through the year, producing colorful flowers in shades of blue, purple, pink, or white. Put plant in an east or west window, or in a south window screened from direct sunlight. Temperature should be about 65 to 70 degrees; if plant is too cool, leaves will turn pale and curl downward. Use a commercial soil mixture or one part each of peat, loam, and sand. Keep soil moist, using warm water; cold spots leaves. Water-soluble fertilizers will spur continual flowering. Plant grows well under fluorescent light. *Natural habitat:* tropical East Africa.

three types of african violet

aluminum plant

Aluminum plant *(Pilea cadierei)* has attractive quilted leaves marked with silver gray. Average potting soil and usual room temperatures are ideal for it. Place plant in a bright place away from direct sunlight and keep soil moderately moist.   *Natural habitat:* tropical Southeast Asia.

Amaryllis *(Hippeastrum)* is striking with its magnificent lilylike flowers in white, pink, or red atop tall stiff stems. Grow it in average potting soil from a bulb planted one-half to one-third above soil level. Keep in a south window, if possible. Water sparingly until flowering stem appears, then gradually increase watering as bud expands. After flowering, feed with fertilizer solution, at half the rate given on the package, for three months to replenish bulb. When leaves turn yellow, reduce watering; then store pot on its side in a cool place. Start growth cycle again in December. Repot in fresh soil about every three years. *Natural habitat:* tropical South Africa.

aphelandra

Aphelandra *(Aphelandra)*, sometimes called zebra plant, is striking with white-veined leaves. Yellow-orange terminal spikes formed by flowers and bracts appear in the fall. It grows best in moist soil with double the usual amount of humus. Give the plant sunlight, but shield it from strong sun of a south window. Keep it slightly pot-bound. Prune plant slightly and rest after bloom fades. *Natural habitat:* Brazil.

Avocado *(Persea americana)* can be grown
from the pit of an avocado pear purchased
in a store. After cutting away the fruit's
edible flesh, wash and dry the pit. Fill a
small glass with water and poke toothpicks
into the sides of the pit so that they will
rest on the edge of the glass and suspend
the pit with its rounded end just touching
the water. When roots form, plant the
pit in potting soil. After the first few leaves
appear, pinch back the growing tip to
encourage branching. Grow plant in a
warm sunny place.

azaleas

Azalea *(Rhododendron)* is a woody plant with pink, red or white flowers and is a popular gift plant. A cool, sunny room is important to keep it thriving. Mist the leaves with warm water daily to increase the humidity. Keep soil moist. After flowers fade, apply an acid-type fertilizer once a month until summer. When repotting, use an acid soil mixture. Some pot-plant varieties are hardy, generally the small-flowered varieties, and these can be planted outdoors in late spring. *Natural habitat:* the cooler regions of the Northern Hemisphere.

kurume azalea
R. obtusum

indian azalea
R. indicum

Baby tears *(Helxine soleirolii)* is a creeping plant with a mass of tiny bright-green leaves on thin intertwining stems. It needs constantly moist, sandy soil and a warm, humid environment. East or west exposure, away from windowsill, is the best location. The plant is a good ground cover in a terrarium or a bottle garden.   *Natural habitat:* the islands of Corsica and Sardinia.

begonias

Begonias *(Begonia)* include more than
6,000 named species and varieties. Most
of these came originally from the forests
of Central and South America. They are
divided into three major groups: tuberous, rhizomatous, and fibrous-rooted.
The latter is the largest and includes
the wax-leafed, angel-wing, and hairy-
leafed types. Generally, the begonias
grow best in a loose humusy soil and in a
pot that keeps them slightly root-bound
without compacting the roots. Allow
the soil to dry out a little between waterings, and avoid any sudden changes in
air temperature. Fertilize plants about
once every three weeks, for continuous
bloom, but not in winter. Keep them in a
south window, but shield them from
the sun's strong rays in summer. Overgrown plants can be kept shapely by
pruning. Clippings can be used to grow
new plants.

tuberous begonia
B. tuberhybrida

metallic-leaf begonia
B. metallica

rex begonia
B. rex

stitch-leaf begonia
B. boweri 'bow-arriola'

wax begonia
B. semperflorens

boxwood

Boxwood *(Buxus microphylla japonica)* is a favorite evergreen garden shrub that is often put in a pot and grown indoors. The soil should be gritty and drain well. Keep boxwood in a cool sunny room, but not in direct sunlight. It grows very slowly. Do not fertilize too often; once every six months is sufficient.   *Natural habitat:* northern Africa and southern Europe.

brazilian edelweiss

Brazilian edelweiss (*Rechsteineria leuco-tricha*) is beguiling with its gray, woolly leaves and rose-colored tubular flowers. Grow it from tubers started in a packaged or homemade soil-less mixture. Water thoroughly, but allow mixture to dry out between waterings. Plant requires bright light or filtered sunlight, warmth, and high humidity. Fertilize regularly every three to four weeks when actively growing. Plants will bloom almost continuously with a brief dormant period in the fall. *Natural habitat:* Brazilian tropics.

Cryptanthus

Aechmea fasciata

Vriesea 'Mariae'

Bromeliads *(Bromeliaceae)* include 1,800 species of magnificently marked plants that are related to the pineapple. Most of them are epiphytes or air plants. They will thrive in the home with modest care. Water must be kept continuously in the "cups" formed by the leaves. Pot them in shallow containers in a fibrous mixture of peat, bark chips, humus, and sand, or use orchid-potting mix. Keep it moist. Apply half the usual amount of fertilizer about twice a year in the potting mix. Bromeliads do best in a large east or west window, but they will grow in north light. Frequent misting keeps foliage clean. Mature plants develop spikes of flowers that last for months. To encourage flowers, place a bromeliad in a plastic bag with a ripe apple for several days. Ethylene gas from the apple initiates flower buds. *Natural habitat:* tropical regions.

cacti and succulents

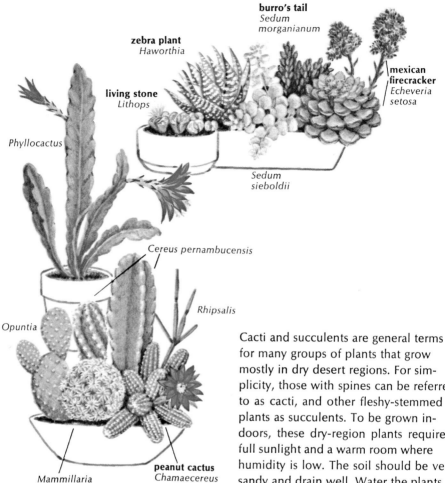

burro's tail
Sedum morganianum

zebra plant
Haworthia

mexican firecracker
Echeveria setosa

living stone
Lithops

Phyllocactus

Sedum sieboldii

Cereus pernambucensis

Rhipsalis

Opuntia

Mammillaria phellosperma

peanut cactus
Chamaecereus silvestri

Cacti and succulents are general terms for many groups of plants that grow mostly in dry desert regions. For simplicity, those with spines can be referred to as cacti, and other fleshy-stemmed plants as succulents. To be grown indoors, these dry-region plants require full sunlight and a warm room where humidity is low. The soil should be very sandy and drain well. Water the plants after they have dried out thoroughly. Assorted species and varieties are suitable for grouping in a desertlike dish garden or growing individually in pots. Be alert for mealy bugs, which are often troublesome. Wipe pests off with a cotton swab dipped in rubbing alcohol. Repeat if they reappear.

88

Caladium *(Caladium)* is a tuberous-rooted plant grown for its spectacularly beautiful leaves, which are splashed with shades of green, cream, pink, red, and white. Most of the leaves are heart-shaped and crepelike in texture. The plants are susceptible to drafts and quick changes of temperature. They should be grown in a warm room where the light is bright; direct sun will fade them.

Start the tubers in the late winter months for spring display, or in the spring months for summer display. Treat them as you would tuberous begonias by starting them in a damp peat moss and soil mixture. When the shoots begin to appear bring them into stronger light and water them more frequently, feeding them monthly. The caladiums can be kept thriving for long seasons, but the tubers should be rested for a month or so by allowing the potting mix to dry out. Repot and water again to start them into growth.   *Natural habitat:* most of the tropical regions of the western hemisphere.

camellia

Camellia *(Camellia)* is an attractive
spring-blooming shrub in the
South, with waxy flowers ranging
in color from white to red. It needs
a bright, sunny, cool place (60
degrees; 40 degrees at night). Use
acid-type fertilizer monthly when
buds are setting, and mist foliage
weekly. Grow it in a fertile soil with
peat moss added. *Natural
habitat:* Asiatic tropics.

chenille plant

Chenille plant *(Acalypha hispida)* has bright-red "fox-tail" flowers set off by green toothed leaves with creamy markings, or deep-maroon leaves with a red border. Place plant in a sunny, warm room and keep its soil evenly moist throughout the growing season. Plants can be pruned hard each spring for summer bloom. Use prunings as cuttings for new plants. *Natural habitat:* tropical India.

chinese evergreen

Chinese evergreen *(Aglaonema modestum)* is a waxy-leaved plant that grows well almost anywhere. It tolerates poor light and low humidity. It can be grown in water containing charcoal chips or in humusy soil kept moist. *Natural habitat:* Southeast Asia.

Christmas cactus *(Schlumbergera bridgesii)*, as its name suggests, blooms around Christmas. Contrary to popular belief, the soil must be kept moist during the growing season, but somewhat dry when the plant is resting. Full sunlight and average room temperatures are recommended. Short days are required to induce blooming. On Sept. 1, plant should have total darkness from 6:00 P.M. to 8:00 A.M. until buds form. Or, if plant is in a cool room (53 degrees), from mid-September to mid-October, flowers will be produced regardless of day length. Most common causes of buds dropping are too high a temperature or too low a light level. A similar plant, *Zygocactus truncatus,* blooms in November. *Natural habitat:* tropical rain forest epiphyte.

christmas pepper

Christmas pepper *(Capsicum annuum conoides)* has
showy red, yellow, or purple peppers in late winter
as its main attraction. Place the plant in a cool
place where it gets full sun. Keep soil constantly
moist. After fruits drop, discard plant, since it is an
annual and will not produce more fruit. Related to
the potato and garden pepper.   *Natural habitat:*
tropical areas.

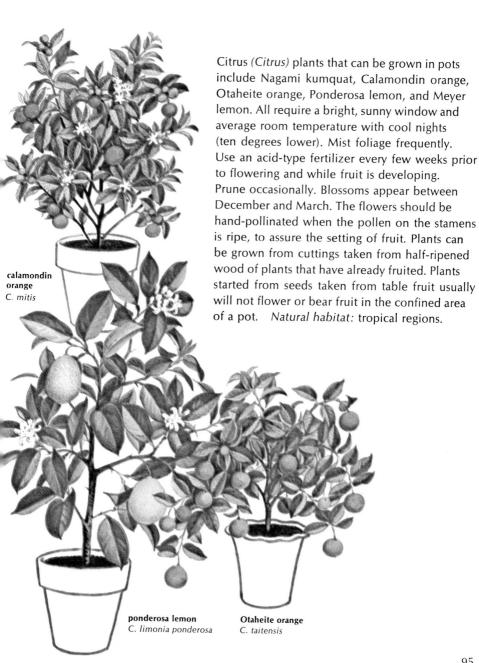

Citrus (*Citrus*) plants that can be grown in pots include Nagami kumquat, Calamondin orange, Otaheite orange, Ponderosa lemon, and Meyer lemon. All require a bright, sunny window and average room temperature with cool nights (ten degrees lower). Mist foliage frequently. Use an acid-type fertilizer every few weeks prior to flowering and while fruit is developing. Prune occasionally. Blossoms appear between December and March. The flowers should be hand-pollinated when the pollen on the stamens is ripe, to assure the setting of fruit. Plants can be grown from cuttings taken from half-ripened wood of plants that have already fruited. Plants started from seeds taken from table fruit usually will not flower or bear fruit in the confined area of a pot. *Natural habitat:* tropical regions.

calamondin orange
C. mitis

ponderosa lemon
C. limonia ponderosa

Otaheite orange
C. taitensis

columnea

Columnea (*Columnea*) has upright forms
as well as trailing forms that are suitable for hanging baskets. Foliage is
velvety, covered with purple hairs. Tubular flowers are red, yellow, or orange
and appear in spring and summer into
fall. Plant needs high humidity, humus-
rich soil, and plenty of sun. Keep soil
moist.   *Natural habitat:* tropical regions.

coral berry

Coral berry *(Ardisia crispa)* is grown
mainly for bright red berries that appear
in fall. No special soil requirements.
Choose a cool, sunny place for the plant
and keep soil moist. Fertilize when actively growing. Discard plant after the
fruit drops since the growing cycle has
ended. In its native tropical climate
of China and Malaya, this plant grows to
a handsome little tree and is prized for
its leathery leaves, which have a polished sheen. Several other species of the
genus *Ardisia* can also be grown indoors
as pot plants.

crotons

Crotons *(Codiaeum)* are bizarre foliage plants with numerous varieties. Mature specimens develop unusual combinations of leaf color in blends of red, pink, cream, yellow, and varying shades of green. Leaves may be oval, elliptical, or oak-leaf shaped. A few varieties have twisted or curled leaves. Plant requires warm temperatures, full sunlight, and evenly moist soil. Be alert to spot and control mealybugs that accumulate in leaf axils. *Natural habitat:* Ceylon and Malaya.

three kinds
of croton

Crown of thorns (*Euphorbia splen-dens*), with small oval leaves and long sharp spines, is a fierce-looking plant. A south window is necessary for best growth. Plant needs sandy soil enriched with humus. It should be watered well and allowed to dry out before watering again; otherwise the leaves drop. Red flowers appear at the tips of branches in winter. *Natural habitat:* Madagascar.

99

cyclamen

Cyclamen (*Cyclamen persicum giganteum*) is prized for its large red, pink, or white flowers. Cool temperatures of 60 to 65 degrees with a 10-degree drop at night are required. Too high a temperature causes leaves to yellow and flower buds to wither. Too little light produces the same results. Keep in an east, west, or south window, preferably a south one. Water regularly. Mist plant daily and keep it on a tray of wet pebbles. If cyclamen mites develop, discard plant as they are difficult to control. *Natural habitat:* Mediterranean region.

Dracaena *(Dracaena)* is a decorative foliage plant that exists in many forms. A slow grower, it tolerates moderate light levels (northern exposure) and low humidity. Keep the soil moist. Grows well in standard potting mixture. Well-known kinds include *D. marginata,* with long, narrow foliage; *D. fragrans massangeana,* often called corn plant, with broad, cornlike leaves; *D. deremensis Warnecki,* with sword-shaped green-and-white-striped leaves; and *D. sanderiana,* a small pot plant.   *Natural habitat:* tropical Africa.

gold-dust dracaena
D. godseffiana

dumb cane

Dumb cane *(Dieffenbachia)* is noted for handsome large leaves with speckled green-and-white markings or veined stripes. It tolerates low humidity and moderate light, but benefits from more of each. Overwatering will rot roots and canes. Let soil dry out moderately between waterings. The plant is toxic, producing painful swelling of the tongue if chewed.   *Natural habitat:* South American tropics.

English ivy *(Hedera helix)* grows best in full sunlight and high humidity. Frequent misting as well as cool temperatures help. Weekly showering of foliage at the sink reduces susceptibility to red spider mites. Pinch back plant frequently to keep it shapely. There are numerous named varieties with unusual leaf shapes and variegations. *Natural habitat:* northern Africa and eastern Asia.

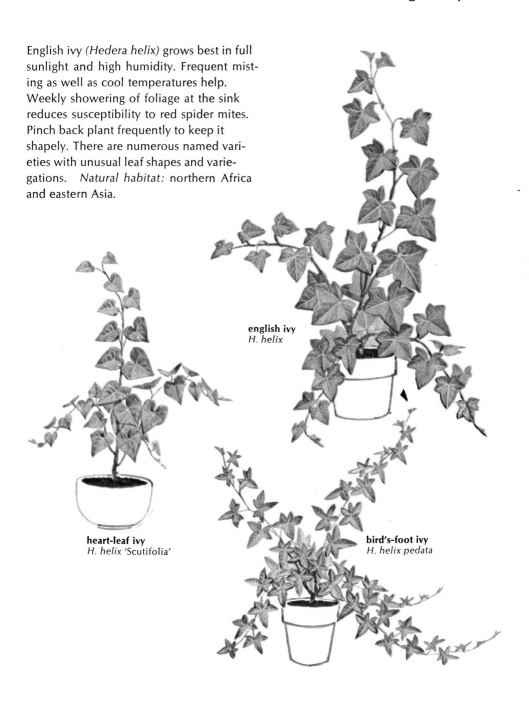

english ivy
H. helix

heart-leaf ivy
H. helix 'Scutifolia'

bird's-foot ivy
H. helix pedata

false aralia

False aralia *(Dizygotheca elegantissima)* has long and narrow-toothed leaves with a leathery texture. It needs bright light, but not direct sunlight. Keep plant in a cool place at 60 to 70 degrees. Allow soil to dry out somewhat between waterings. Large plants are difficult to acclimatize in the low humidity of home environment.   *Natural habitat:* New Hebrides in the South Pacific.

Fatshedera (*Fatshedera lizei*) is a bige-
neric cross between English ivy and
fatsia. It has thick evergreen leaves like
ivy. Its stems may need support for
upright growth. Plant requires an east
or west exposure, a fertile soil enriched
with humus, and a cool temperature of
50 to 70 degrees. One of the varieties
of this hybrid, *F. lizei variegata,* has
handsomely decorative foliage with
cream-white markings that contrast
sharply against its dark-green background.

105

fatsia

Fatsia *(Fatsia japonica),* from Japan, is a
handsome foliage plant with leathery
maplelike leaves. It grows best in east or
west light and constantly moist soil.
Fertilize it monthly and keep it in a cool
place. *Natural habitat:* Japan.

Ferns *(Polypodiaceae)* best for indoors are Boston *(Nephrolepsis)*, coarse-leaved polypody *(Polypodium)*, brake *(Pteris)*, bird's-nest *(Asplenium nidus)*, maidenhair *(Adiantum)*, and rabbit's-foot *(Davallia)*. These require warmth, high humidity, good light (but not direct sunlight), and deep, frequent watering. A porous soil or fibrous growing medium that drains quickly is essential. Small, raised dots or lines that appear on the undersides or margins of the fronds contain spores, the reproductive bodies of ferns.

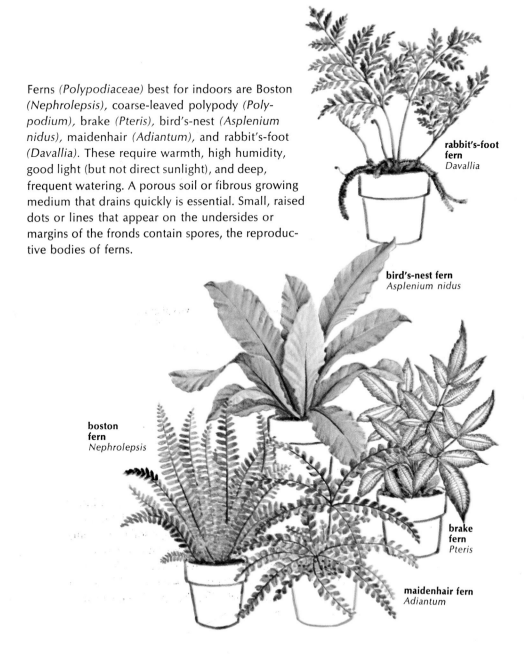

rabbit's-foot fern
Davallia

bird's-nest fern
Asplenium nidus

boston fern
Nephrolepsis

brake fern
Pteris

maidenhair fern
Adiantum

figs

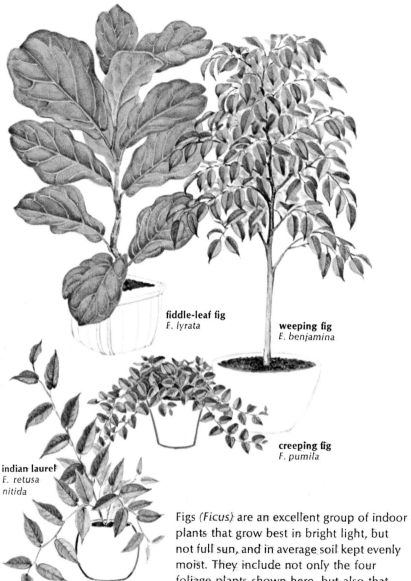

fiddle-leaf fig
F. lyrata

weeping fig
E. benjamina

creeping fig
F. pumila

indian laurel
*E. retusa
nitida*

Figs *(Ficus)* are an excellent group of indoor plants that grow best in bright light, but not full sun, and in average soil kept evenly moist. They include not only the four foliage plants shown here, but also that old favorite, the India rubber plant (page 117). The species grown for fruit is *Ficus carica,* a subtropical tree which will bear fruit only outdoors.

Fittonia (*Fittonia*) is a showy foliage plant that grows as a groundcover in Peru. Its leaves are oval, with netted red or white veining. They will wilt unless humus-rich soil is kept constantly moist. Plant grows well in a terrarium or wherever humidity is high. It needs a bright east or west window, but not full sun. Feed every six weeks.

flame violet

Flame violet *(Episcia)* is noted for its foliage as well as its everblooming orange-red flowers. It requires about the same care as African violet does. Plant needs warm environment; its leaves blacken if temperature falls below 55 degrees. For best bloom, keep light humusy soil constantly moist and provide high humidity by misting plant regularly. Fertilize every two weeks when growing actively. There are many varieties with distinctively marked foliage. One species, *E. dianthiflora,* has small leaves and large white flowers. *Natural habitat:* tropical America.

flowering maple

Flowering maple *(Abutilon)* has maplelike variegated leaves. Its hanging bell-
like flowers are white, yellow, apricot,
pink, or red. Blooms intermittently.
Put it in a bright window and keep its
soil moist, slightly drier in winter. Pinch
back young shoots when inches high
to induce branching. Prune mature
plants in winter to improve their shape.
Natural habitat: tropical South America.

fuchsia

Fuchsia *(Fuchsia)*, also called lady's eardrops, includes
many excellent hybrids that have beautiful bell-like
flowers and showy stamens. Colors are in shades of pink,
red, rose, blue, and fuchsia, as well as white. Sunlight,
part of the day, and good air circulation are needed for
plants to bloom well. Fertilize every two weeks when
flowering and prune plants to keep them shapely. Soil
should be dried during the winter resting period. Fuchsias
are ideal for hanging baskets.   *Natural habitat:* tropical
America.

Gardenia *(Gardenia)* needs full sunlight for growth of its dark, glossy leaves and development of its handsome, waxy flowers which appear most of the year. But it should be shaded from the strong summer sun. Normal indoor temperature suits it during the day and night until flower buds form. Then a five- or ten-degree drop at night is important; otherwise, flower buds may drop. Use acid-type fertilizer containing iron; deficiency of iron causes yellow leaves. Fertilize every few weeks when buds are setting. Keep acid soil moist and mist plant frequently.   *Natural habitat:* tropical regions.

geranium

Geranium *(Pelargonium)* does best in soil that has a high clay content (two parts clay to one of sand and humus). Soil too rich in nitrogen promotes all leaf growth and no flowers, as does overfertilizing. Let soil dry out between waterings and keep plant in full sunlight. Overwatering causes leaves to turn yellow. Cool night temperature aids flowering. Geraniums will bloom almost year-round. *Natural habitat:* semiarid regions of southern Africa.

Gloxinia *(Sinningia speciosa)* is grown for
its spectacular trumpet flowers with
red, blue, or white petals, often speckled.
Plant tubers in February in packaged or
homemade soil-less mixture that is
kept moist in a warm location. To bloom
in spring, the plant needs moderate sun
and high humidity. Frequent misting is
beneficial. Avoid any sudden temperature change. After flowering, continue
growing plant until leaves wane. Gradually withhold water and store dormant
tubers in pot. Repot them again in
February for rebloom. Fertilize regularly
every two weeks. *Natural habitat:*
Brazilian tropics.

grape ivy

Grape ivy *(Cissus rhombifolia)* grows well in poor light and with little care as long as its soil is kept moist. Pinch back plant to keep it shapely. Vine has three-part leaves, and tendrils for climbing. *Natural habitat:* West Indies and tropical America.

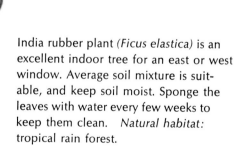

India rubber plant *(Ficus elastica)* is an excellent indoor tree for an east or west window. Average soil mixture is suitable, and keep soil moist. Sponge the leaves with water every few weeks to keep them clean. *Natural habitat:* tropical rain forest.

117

jade plant

Jade plant *(Crassula argentea)* is a sturdy, thick-stemmed plant with fleshy leaves. It needs about six hours of sunlight daily. Insufficient sunlight is the chief cause of the plant's failure to thrive. Soil should include enough sand to make it feel gritty and should be enriched with humus. Let soil dry out thoroughly before each watering. *Natural habitat:* South Africa.

jerusalem cherry

Jerusalem cherry *(Solanum pseudo-capsicum)* is popular during the holiday season because of its red fruits (which are poisonous). Keep it in a sunny room and allow its soil to dry out slightly between waterings. Since plant is an annual and will not flower again, discard it after fruit drops. *Natural habitat:* Madeira.

kafir lily

Kafir lily *(Clivia miniata)* is a handsome plant from southern Africa that is exceptionally beautiful in bloom. Only mature plants, several years of age, flower. Trumpet-shaped blossoms in orange, scarlet, or salmon appear in spring. Plant requires a large pot, soil enriched with bone meal, a partly sunny location, and a cool temperature (50 to 65 degrees). Water sparingly in winter. Keep it pot-bound.

kalanchoe

Kalanchoe *(Kalanchoe)* is an unusual group of succulents that includes the air plant *(K. pinnata)* and the fuzzy-leafed panda plant *(K. tomentosa)*. Keep them in a cool place but in full sunlight. Too little light causes ungainly growth. Use a sandy soil mix and water thoroughly. Allow to dry out between waterings. Plants bloom in December if the length of their day is shortened during September by giving them complete darkness from 6:00 P.M. to 7:00 A.M.   *Natural habitat:* Madagascar and tropical Africa.

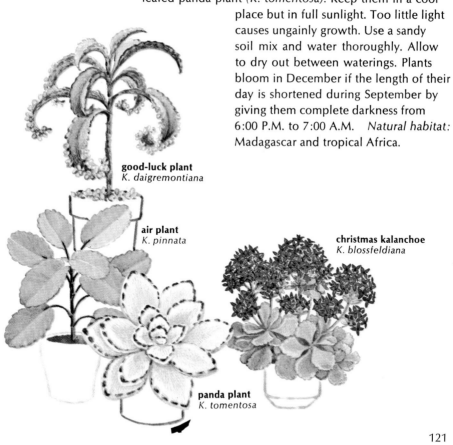

good-luck plant
K. daigremontiana

air plant
K. pinnata

christmas kalanchoe
K. blossfeldiana

panda plant
K. tomentosa

kangaroo vine

Kangaroo vine *(Cissus antarctica)* is a large-leafed trailing plant related to grape ivy. It will grow easily in average soil that is kept moist, either in or out of sunlight.   *Natural habitat:* tropical.

kohleria

Kohleria *(Kohleria)* features speckled tubular flowers in orange, scarlet, or pink atop upright stems against a background of large, velvety leaves. Grow plant from a tuber started in a packaged or home-made soil-less mixture that is kept moist. A partly sunny location is best. When growth wanes, cut plant to soil level; tuber will resprout. After a dry-soil resting period, usually several weeks, fertilize the plant every few weeks to boost new growth. *Natural habitat:* tropical America.

lipstick plant

Lipstick plant *(Aeschynanthus lobbianus)* is a trailing plant with dark-green waxy leaves, brightened by orange or red tubular flowers which bloom almost year-round in terminal clusters. Keep it in a warm, humid site (a sunny bathroom is ideal). Cut back its trailing stems after flowering. Pot in a mixture of one part each vermiculite, peat, and perlite. Fertilize every three weeks.   *Natural habitat:* Southeast Asia.

Moses-in-the-cradle *(Rhoeo spathacea)*
is so named for its unusual blooms that
are borne on swordlike leaves off and on
during the year. Easy to grow, it does
well at average house temperatures and
in north or brighter light. Use average
potting soil and keep it moist. *Natural
habitat:* Mexico.

myrtle

Myrtle *(Myrtus)* is a small woody shrub that grows nicely in a pot. Keep it in sunlight, but in a cool room. Water it thoroughly, but allow soil to dry out before next watering. Prune plant to keep it shapely. It may bloom if conditions are ideal. Slow growing; hence requires little or no fertilizers. *Natural habitat:* Mediterranean region.

Nautilocalyx *(Nautilocalyx)* is a group of plants with showy foliage. They require warm temperatures, sun, and high humidity. To be sure the potting mixture drains well and retains moisture, use a soil-less mixture like that recommended for gloxinia. *Natural habitat:* Peru.

norfolk island pine

Norfolk Island pine (*Araucaria excelsa*) is an evergreen, but not a true pine, from an island near New Zealand. It can be grown as a pot plant when young. Average soil must be kept moist. Plant endures low humidity, but must have east or west sunlight or it becomes misshapen.

Orchids *(Orchidaceae)* include thousands of species and hybrids from tropical regions around the world. Many can be grown in the home if provided with bright sunlight, high humidity (from daily misting), and a moisture-retaining growing medium such as osmunda bark. Some orchids do best in cool temperatures, others in warm. The plant may flower for a month or more and then go through a long dormancy period. Many bloom and grow well under fluorescent lamps. A few of the easier-to-grow types are *Cattleya, Epidendrum, Oncidium,* and *Phalaenopsis.*

Epidendrum radicans

Dendrobium nobile

moth orchid
Phalaenopsis amabilis

Cattleya

pansy orchid
Miltonia

oxalis

Oxalis *(Oxalis)* is a cloverlike plant, of wide natural distribution, whose flowers and leaves close up at night. Full sunlight and a cool room promote plant vigor and longer-lasting blooms. Grow oxalis from bulbs planted in a soil mixture of two parts clay to one each of sand and humus. Water soil well, but allow it to dry off between waterings. Fertilize every month while blooming. Gradually reduce watering after flowering to induce dormancy. Repot when the multiplying bulbs become overcrowded. *Natural habitat:* warm or tropical regions.

Palm *(Palmaceae)* includes many varieties suitable for growing in houses as ornamental foliage plants. The main reason for failure in growing them is poor environment. Palms should be kept away from sunlight, but they need warmth. Their soil should be a mixture of two parts clay to one each of sand and humus; it should be kept moist at all times. Syringe foliage occasionally to keep it clean; sponge off larger plants. Do not overfertilize. *Natural habitat:* tropical.

peacock plant

Peacock plant *(Calathea makoyana) is* grown for its highly decorative foliage. It needs a warm location and moist soil. Frequent misting helps to maintain high humidity. Keep plant away from direct sunlight, but in a bright location. *Natural habitat:* Brazilian tropics.

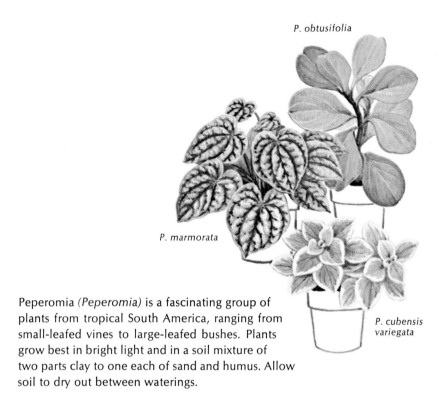

P. obtusifolia

P. marmorata

P. cubensis
variegata

Peperomia *(Peperomia)* is a fascinating group of
plants from tropical South America, ranging from
small-leafed vines to large-leafed bushes. Plants
grow best in bright light and in a soil mixture of
two parts clay to one each of sand and humus. Allow
soil to dry out between waterings.

philodendron

Philodendron *(Philodendron)* is one of the largest plant groups suitable for indoors. There are erect and vine types, all having attractive foliage. They grow well in average soil enriched with humus, and in filtered or indirect light. Too little light causes leaves of some types to grow smaller and smaller. Keep soil evenly moist and add water-soluble plant fertilizer two or three times a year. Prune vine types occasionally, just above a leaf. *Natural habitat:* tropical America.

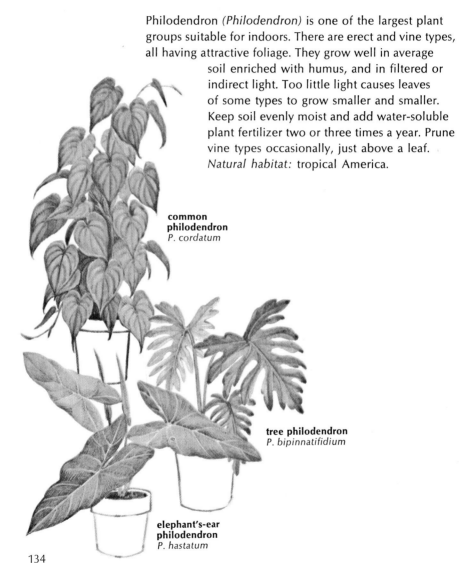

**common
philodendron**
P. cordatum

tree philodendron
P. bipinnatifidium

**elephant's-ear
philodendron**
P. hastatum

piggyback plant

Piggyback plant *(Tolmiea menziesii)* has somewhat fuzzy leaves. Tiny plantlets that form in bases of leaves and give plant its name can be rooted. Pot in average soil and keep it evenly moist. Be alert for mealybugs. *Natural habitat:* western North America.

pittosporum

Pittosporum *(Pittosporum tobira)* is a tropical tree with thick, shiny leaves. Plant
grows best indoors in average soil when
the room temperature is quite cool (50
to 55 degrees). Place it in sunlight and keep
its soil on the dry side. Prune often to
keep it shapely. Feed once or twice a year.

Poinsettia (*Euphorbia pulcherrima*) is prized for its colorful red bracts produced around Christmastime. These red bracts, contrary to popular belief, are not flowers but leaves. The true flowers are the little nubs in the center of the bracts. The bracts last longer if the plant is kept in a sunny site free from drafts. Water it well. Because poinsettias become unattractively leggy toward spring and rebloom in winter only if day length is controlled, they are most often discarded after the holidays. To successfully keep plants for another year, the foliage is kept growing after bracts drop. Cut back plant and place outdoors for summer. Repot and bring the plant indoors by September 1. From October 1 to late November, poinsettias must have complete darkness from 5:00 P.M. to 8:00 A.M. for flower-bud set. *Natural habitat:* Mexico.

polyscias

Polyscias *(Polyscias)* is a woody-stemmed plant with attractive leaves that sometimes have white, gray, or green variegation. Needs fresh air and a sunny, warm room. Does not need direct sun. It does well in average soil kept uniformly moist. *Natural habitat:* South Pacific islands.

Pothos *(Scindapsus)* resembles *Philodendron* except its leaves are lighter in color and usually variegated. It is an excellent plant for poorly lit corners and a dry atmosphere. Soak its soil thoroughly and allow soil to dry out between waterings. The plant can be trained to climb on bark. Frequent showering under the faucet with warm water will keep the leaves clean and promote good foliage growth. *Natural habitat:* eastern Asia.

prayer plant

Prayer plant (*Maranta leuconeura ker-choveana*) is so named because its unusually marked gray-green leaves with brown blotches fold upward at night like praying hands. Place plant where it gets partial shade and keep soil moist. Frequent misting helps to maintain needed high humidity. A few other species of the genus *Maranta* are grown as house plants. Most were found in the tropical rain forests of Brazil and grow best in soil enriched with peat or compost.

Screw pine *(Pandanus)*, not a true pine, is an old-
fashioned plant with leaves that have finely serrated,
sharp edges, like sawblades. Grow it in a loamy soil
mixture that drains well. Keep in a warm place
near, but not in, an east or west window. Let soil
dry out between waterings. Repot when plant
becomes root-bound. *Natural habitat:* tropics of
Malaysia.

shrimp plant

Shrimp plant *(Beloperone guttata)* has hanging clusters of orange-coppery bracts, which resemble shrimp, terminated by white flowers appearing all summer into fall. It is a woody plant that needs frequent pinching back to keep it shapely. Grow it at room temperature in full sunlight. Water frequently. *Natural habitat:* Mexico.

Singapore holly *(Malpighia coccigera)* has small, shiny, rounded leaves that resemble leaves of boxwood; some mature leaves have spines suggesting holly. Its flowers are small, pale pink, much like pinwheels and appear infrequently. Allow plant's soil to dry out before each watering. Bright light and average room temperature are recommended. Those who visit in the subtropical regions will recognize this plant as a hedge used in formal garden settings. The young shoots root easily in sand and peat moss. An excellent plant to train as bonsai. Do not overfeed. *Natural habitat:* West Indies.

sinningia

Sinningia *(Sinningia pusilla)* is one of the smallest plants grown indoors. It fits in a teacup and grows nicely in a brandy snifter. The flowers are miniatures, too. It needs high humidity, sunlight and preferably a soil-less potting mixture. Larger tuberous hybrids are available. *Natural habitat:* Brazilian tropics.

snake plant

Snake plant *(Sansevieria)*, a favorite of yesteryear
with numerous species and varieties, endures
neglect, limited light, and dry soil. Mature plants
in sunny rooms often send up spikes of white
blooms. *Natural habitat:* Africa.

S. hahnii

S. trifasciata

southern yew

Southern yew *(Podocarpus)* is a hardy outdoor
shrub in southern states and a pot plant in northern
climates. It grows best in a cool place (50 to 55
degrees) that gets indirect light. Prune it often.
Soil should be kept moderately moist.

Spathe flower *(Spathiphyllum)* has green glossy leaves and sometimes produces unusual white blossoms but its main feature is its foliage. Leaves scorch in too much sunlight. Plant thrives in a warm room with filtered light. Keep soil constantly moist. *Natural habitat:* Central America.

spider plant

Spider plant *(Chlorophytum)* is so named because mature plants develop long wiry stems, at the end of which small plants develop. A popular hanging-basket plant, it grows best in bright, indirect light and constantly moist soil. Fertilize it once a month. *Natural habitat:* South Africa.

strawberry geranium

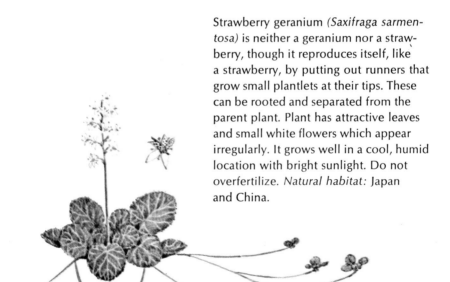

Strawberry geranium (*Saxifraga sarmentosa*) is neither a geranium nor a strawberry, though it reproduces itself, like a strawberry, by putting out runners that grow small plantlets at their tips. These can be rooted and separated from the parent plant. Plant has attractive leaves and small white flowers which appear irregularly. It grows well in a cool, humid location with bright sunlight. Do not overfertilize. *Natural habitat:* Japan and China.

streptocarpus

Streptocarpus *(Streptocarpus)*, also called Cape primrose, originates near the Cape of Good Hope in South Africa. It is an ungainly plant with very long quilted leaves, but its blue, violet, or white flowers are worthwhile. It grows well in a south, east, or west window if soil is kept moist. It usually is started from seed in winter and blooms the next winter for several months. After blooming it has a two- to three-month dormancy period. To break the dormancy period, water and feed to encourage new growth.

sweet olive

Sweet olive *(Osmanthus fragrans)* is an evergreen Asiatic tree that can be grown as a pot plant when small. It has dark shiny leaves and clusters of tiny, fragrant white flowers that bloom all year. Keep it in a cool place that gets direct sunlight. Soil should have high clay content, but drain well. Keep it evenly moist and fertilize monthly. This plant is frequently grown in semitropical gardens as a hedge or specimen shrub where thick, dense growth is needed.

swiss cheese plant

Swiss cheese plant *(Monstera deliciosa)*
is so named because its large mature
leaves are dotted with holes (or sometimes slashed). Plant thrives in poor light;
low humidity retards its growth. Keep
foliage clean by washing with a damp
sponge. Soak soil thoroughly at least
once a week or oftener.   *Natural
habitat:* tropical Mexico.

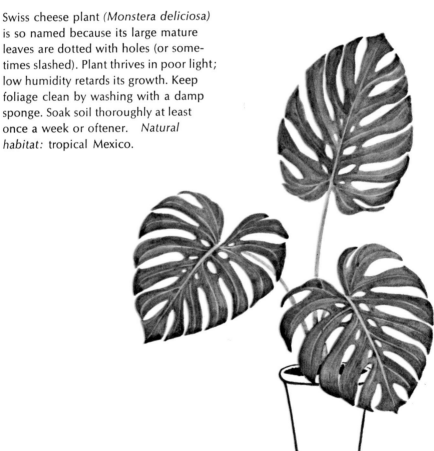

Syngonium *(Syngonium)* is a fine indoor foliage plant. Its beautifully marked green-and-white leaves are either shaped like an arrowhead or are three-parted. All forms will grow well in limited light exposures and in a humus-rich soil kept evenly moist. *Natural habitat:* Central America.

temple bells

Temple bells *(Smithiantha)* is popular for its velvety red-green foliage with nodding bell-like flowers that bloom from late summer to midwinter. It is grown from a rhizome (underground stem). Plant needs high humidity, filtered sunlight, and preferably a soil-less potting mixture. After bloom, allow potting mixture to dry off and keep it barely moist for rhizome rest period. There are several named hybrids of this handsome plant now available. They have unusually brilliant flowers and the typical rich, velvety foliage. The original species from which the hybrids were developed were discovered growing wild in the tropical regions of Guatemala and Mexico. Requires moderate feeding.

ti plant

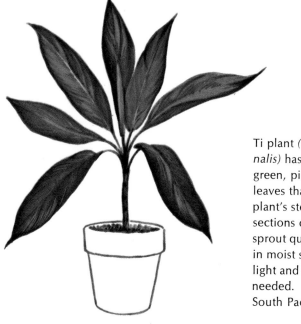

Ti plant *(Cordyline termi-nalis)* has red, maroon, deep-green, pink, or variegated leaves that spiral up the plant's stem. Inch-long sections of the stem will sprout quickly when placed in moist sand. East or west light and moist soil are needed. *Natural habitat:* South Pacific islands.

umbrella plant

Umbrella plant *(Cyperus alternifolius)* takes its name from long, slender leaflets that stand atop a sturdy stem like an umbrella. Related to Egyptian papyrus, this plant needs constantly wet soil and should be kept in a saucer filled with water. It grows best in full sunlight and cool surroundings. The species is a native of the island of Madagascar where it grows in wetlands. A dwarf form is available.

umbrella tree

Umbrella tree *(Brassaia actino-phylla) or Schefflera* is a rapidly developing decorative plant grown in average soil. Sponge leaves often to keep them clean. Let soil dry out between waterings. Excessive dryness or wetness causes leaves to drop. Plant needs sunlight, but tolerates some shade and low humidity. *Natural habitat:* Australia.

velvet plant

Velvet plant *(Gynura aurantiaca)* features clusters of orange flowers set off by soft-textured, deep-purple leaves which appear occasionally. Plant needs sunlight and moist soil enriched with humus. Requires moderate feeding. *Natural habitat:* Java.

Wandering jew *(Tradescantia)* is a tropical trailing plant that is excellent for hanging baskets. It is easy to grow in average potting soil or in water with charcoal chips. Plant requires indirect light and warmth.

wax plant

Wax plant *(Hoya)* is available in many species with variations in leaf shapes and patterns, some variegated. An excellent vine with waxy white flower

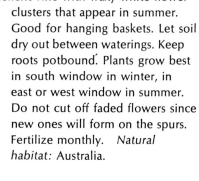

clusters that appear in summer. Good for hanging baskets. Let soil dry out between waterings. Keep roots potbound. Plants grow best in south window in winter, in east or west window in summer. Do not cut off faded flowers since new ones will form on the spurs. Fertilize monthly. *Natural habitat:* Australia.

unusual plants

anthurium

Anthurium (*Anthurium*) is grown for its large, waxy leaves which are brightly colored in tones of red or pink. Some species have velvety green leaves with white veining. All are heart-shaped and may range in size from less than a foot to several feet long. The flower has an odd appearance with its drooping, tail-like structure. These exotic-looking plants come from the dense, tropical, forest regions of Central America, a climate difficult to duplicate in the home atmosphere, but more readily attainable in a greenhouse.

   Pot the anthuriums in orchid fiber, leafmold, or sphagnum moss. They must be kept in a constantly moist atmosphere, and the growing medium must always be kept damp. Feed them once every four weeks with a water-soluble fertilizer. Keep them in warm room temperatures during the day. Temperatures should never go below 55 degrees at night. *Natural habitat:* forests of Central America.

asparagus

Asparagus (*Asparagus*) is a species of asparagus not even related to ferns. Its feathery appearance is due to its many tiny branchlets, not really leaves at all. (In the species *sprengeri,* the leaves have been reduced to thorns.) These plants are delightful for hanging baskets and grow well in bright light, but not direct sunlight. The plants have fleshy-type roots and grow best in average soil with peat moss added. Keep turning hanging plants every week or so to keep them well shaped. Soak thoroughly when watering, then allow soil to dry out a bit before watering again. If growing conditions are ideal, short-lived tiny pink flowers will appear, followed by red berries which contain seeds. Plant the seeds for more plants. *Natural habitat:* dry regions of South Africa.

cape cowslip

Cape cowslip *(Lachenalia)* is a delightful tender bulb from South Africa that should be grown more often. The bell-like flowers hang from a spike about a foot tall and are in shades of yellow touched with red, purple, or lavender. The leaves circle the base somewhat like those of a hyacinth. Bulbs are planted in the fall in average soil, several of them to a three- or four-inch pot. Until the leaves appear above the soil, keep it just barely moist. Then, as growth begins, water regularly and put the pot in full sun. After flowers fade, keep the foliage growing until it begins to yellow. Dry off gradually and store the bulbs for next year in a dark cool place. If there is no space to leave them stored in their pots you may remove them and store them in a plastic bag again in a dark cool place. Start the cycle again in fall.

carissa

Carissa *(Carissa)* is sometimes called Natal plum. A spiny evergreen shrub in its native South Africa, it can be grown successfully in pots. The leathery, oval-shaped leaves are deep green, and delightfully fragrant, white, star-shaped flowers appear intermittently throughout the year. If left undisturbed, small, red, plumlike fruits will develop. The plant will grow well in average potting soil in a cool room. An east or west window is best. Water well, allowing the soil to dry out a bit in between. Prune to keep the plant shapely.

crossandra

Crossandra (*Crossandra*) is a delightful, summer-blooming plant with long, oval leaves and bright-red tubular flowers. The plant is sometimes called the "firecracker flower." The plant grows well in average soil, kept moist. Keep in a warm room, away from drafts and in bright light. Do not overfertilize. *Natural habitat:* India and Ceylon.

dipladenia

Dipladenia (*Dipladenia*) is becoming popular for its beautiful funnel-shaped flowers resembling petunias. A vinelike woody plant with glossy leaves, it grows vigorously if kept in bright light. Keep the soil constantly moist, and enrich heavy clay-soil mixture with a generous amount of peat moss or rotted compost. If growing conditions are ideal, the blooms will continue to appear during most of the year. Feed regularly during the active growing season, once every three or four weeks. *Natural habitat:* tropical South America.

german ivy

German ivy (*Senecio mikanioides*) is an old-fashioned plant that is making a comeback. Often called "parlor ivy," its leaves resemble those of the true ivy (*Hedera*), but they are lighter in color and texture. The plant does well in hanging baskets. During the winter months it can be in a sunny window, but during the summer keep it away from direct sunlight. Keep it cool, the soil (average potting soil) moist, and fertilize about every four to six weeks. Keep plant trimmed and shapely; root cuttings to make new plants. Hanging planters can be kept outdoors in a shady place during the summer months. *Natural habitat:* South Africa.

glory bowers

Glory bowers (*Clerodendrum thomsonae*) is a vigorous tropical vine from the Congo region of West Africa. The unusual crimson flowers have creamy-white outer petals. The leaves are large—up to five inches—and papery in texture. In ideal conditions the vine can take over the corner of a greenhouse.

Confined to pot culture, it can be kept under control. Give the vine full sun and pot it in average soil kept moist. A rest period during the gray winter months helps; just cut down on the watering. Pinch back the straggly stems to keep it trim.

hydrangea

Hydrangea (*Hydrangea macrophylla*) is a popular pot plant for gift giving at Easter and Mother's Day. The plant does nicely in the house for a few brief weeks, but thrives out of doors or planted in the garden. It has large, ball-shaped flower clusters massed above large papery leaves and requires regular watering so the soil (average potting soil) is always moist to the touch. Flowering will last for six weeks or so in spring. After flowering, cut back and plant in a sunny place in the garden where the soil drains well. Lime in the soil will keep future flowers pink; alum in the soil will keep future flowers blue. These materials are added once during the growing months in summer and again in early spring. *Natural habitat:* widely distributed.

impatiens

Impatiens (*Impatiens*) are succulent-stemmed, showy garden plants that adapt to pot culture easily. They are from the mountainous regions of Africa and New Guinea and are grown for their spectacularly bright flowers in shades of rose, pink, white, and orange. Some people call this "patience plant" or "patient Lucy." The plant grows easily from seed, or cuttings from garden plants can be rooted in late summer and brought indoors to pot as house plants. *Impatiens* is also ideal for hanging baskets. Grow in average soil and fertilize every two to three weeks when growing actively. Keep in direct sun in winter, but in an east or west window in summer. (In the garden, the plant prefers a shady area.) Bloom usually continues the year round.

lantana

Lantana (*Lantana*) is a woody-stemmed plant with verbena-like flowers in shades of red, orange, yellow, and pink. The leaves are rough-textured with a rather pungent, distinctive odor. It's a spectacular summer-blooming plant, with some flowering continuing into the winter months. Adaptable in growing habit, it can be grown as a pot plant, a standard, or a hanging-basket plant. *Lantana* is highly susceptible to red spider and white fly, and frequent syringing of the foliage is a good preventative. Grow in average potting soil, kept moist, and feed every two to three weeks when actively growing. Keep in bright sunlight except during the winter months when it rests somewhat. Cuttings of garden plants can be rooted for pot plants indoors. *Natural habitat:* tropical.

lily of the valley

Lily of the valley *(Convallaria majalis)* can be forced in the same manner as hardy bulbs. The "pips," or growth buds, are prechilled before commercial sale and are then potted in a bowl of peat moss that is kept moist and placed in a cool, bright place. Green tips start to come up and flowers appear in about three weeks. Keep the foliage green and growing, then plant them in the garden or give them to friends who have a garden. Home gardeners should not try to dig up and force their own lily of the valley as the pips are specially grown and treated commercially for forcing. A five-inch pot will accommodate a dozen pips since they must be planted close together for best display.

pellionia

Pellionia *(Pellionia)* is a fine hanging-basket plant with purple-tinted, black-veined leaves. The stems are purple, too, making it a fascinating foliage attraction. It is a creeper that hugs its container and grows in a slow drooping fashion. Keep it potted in a fibrous potting mixture which must always be moist to the touch. An unusual plant, it may be difficult to find, but is sometimes available from specialty florists with their own greenhouses. *Natural habitat:* South Vietnam.

purple heart

Purple heart (*Setcreasea purpurea*) has fleshy, lance-shaped leaves which appear purple in bright sun-light. During the summer and early fall, it has tiny lilac flowers in between the leaves. The plant requires average soil that is kept moist. Summer the plants outdoors if possible, or keep them out of too bright sunlight indoors during July and August. *Natural habitat:* Mexico.

rhipsalis

Rhipsalis (*Rhipsalis*) is a fascinating group of epiphytic cacti that make excellent hanging plants. Their leaves are slim, rounded, and pencil-like, hanging in long strands. Mature plants will flower, then produce small globular fruits that suggest mistletoe. The plants must be grown in a porous mixture of half peat and half humus, or in orchid-potting fiber. Be sure the pot drains well and always allow soil to dry out between waterings. As with all cacti types, full sun, if possible, is best. These tree epiphytes can be found in many parts of the world.

sapphire flower

Sapphire flower (*Browallia*) is a delightful hanging-basket plant to brighten a sunny room. The lovely, starlike blooms appear most of the year. It can also be grown as a pot plant and kept in a sunny east or west window where the temperatures are on the cool side. Fertilize the plant once every two to three weeks and pinch back if it becomes straggly. Cuttings are easy to root in vermiculite or perlite. Pot them in average potting soil. *Natural habitat:* Columbia, tropical America.

swedish ivy

Swedish ivy (*Plectranthus australis*) is a leathery-leaved trailing plant from Australia that is ideal for hanging baskets. It is not a true ivy, but related to the mints. White blossoms will appear during the summer months. The plant should be grown in average soil which has been lightened with either vermiculite or perlite. Keep the soil moist to the touch and grow the plant in good light, but not

166

direct sunlight, especially in the summer months. It can be summered outdoors.

string of hearts

String of hearts *(Ceropegia woodii)* is a trailing succulent from Rhodesia, so named because it has tiny, heart-shaped leaves hanging on long, pendant stems. The plant grows well in hanging baskets and its somewhat glossy-gray color adds a unique decorative accent. During the summer months, dainty pink flowers string along the stems. The plant should be rested during the winter months by allowing the sandy soil to dry out gradually for a month or so. Tiny tubers develop along the stems where the leaves are attached. These may be cut off and planted.

taffeta plant

Taffeta plant *(Hoffmannias)* is aptly named—the leaves do look like big pieces of showy green taffeta. They are oblong in shape with a green-brown cast and very deep veins—some even have a quilted look. When conditions are ideal, these are excellent display pot plants. Grow them in a good, moist soil mixture that drains well, and keep the plants in bright light but out of drafts. Frequent misting will help to keep humidity around them high. *Natural habitat:* tropical Mexico.

digging
deeper
into
house
plants

gardening under lights

Electricity opens new horizons in indoor plant growing. With the flick of a switch, any bookshelf, basement, dark corner, or kitchen cupboard can become a plant-growing center. Fluorescent lamps with reflectors and high-intensity incandescent bulbs are making it possible to have indoor gardens where none otherwise could exist.

Not all house plants, however, can be grown under artificial light. Since this light is not nearly as intense as sunlight, it will support only plants that require no more than moderate sunlight. Plants that grow well under artificial light include *Achimenes,* African violet, Brazilian edelweiss, *Columnea,* flame violet, gloxinia, *Kohleria,* lipstick plant, *Nautilocalyx, Sinningia, Streptocarpus,* and temple bells. Ferns do fine, and so do some cacti and succulents. Begonias thrive, and orchids flower nicely. Some growers now seem to have moderate success with herbs and even a few vegetable crops, such as lettuce.

A table lamp gives sufficient light to boost the growth of foliage plants such as philoden-

dron, English ivy, and pothos. If such a lamp is
kept lighted four to five hours a day, the plants
will grow exceptionally well. A 150-watt spot-
light or floodlight may be used above a tall indoor tree. A high ceiling is required for this
setup, however, for the light must be four feet
above the top of the foliage.

For most plant setups, fluorescent lamps are
best. They provide more growing space under
them and have the higher light intensities required by many plants. Fluorescent light is
cooler, more even, and cheaper than incandescent light.

It is excellent not only for growing mature
plants, but also for raising seedlings and propagating cuttings. A gardener can raise annuals
and vegetable plants in early spring so that they
are ready to be set in the ground outdoors as
soon as the weather settles. Keep the lamps
three to four inches above the sprouting seedlings and raise the lamps as the seedlings grow
taller. Cuttings of both house plants and some
woody shrubs can also be rooted with the aid of
fluorescent light.

Fluorescent lamps are available in white, cool
white, warm white, natural, and daylight. These
terms define the amount of coloring in the
tubes, not their temperature. Plants need mostly
red light for root growth and blue light for stem
and leaf growth. A combination of one cool
white (largely red) tube and one daylight
(largely blue) tube supplies a well-balanced
light spectrum for indoor plants. (To raise seedlings, use only warm-white tubes, which are
especially rich in red rays.)

More costly but often worth the expense are
the newly improved agricultural or "growth"

173

The alcove between two bookcases with its small cupboard below becomes a fern greenery with the addition of lights.

One wall in a city apartment becomes dramatically effective with the installation of shelves and lamps for plant growing. Lateral strips conceal the lamp mountings from view.

A skillful amateur carpenter designed and built cabinets and wall hangers to transform a sunroom into an indoor greenery. Doors on the lighted cabinet are closed to increase humidity.

174

lamps (sold under various trade names) which now provide in a single tube the full range of the light spectrum needed for plant growth. They look like natural light, but are stronger in intensity.

Many prefabricated plant-growing stands, some with wheels, can be bought, complete with growing trays and fluorescent fixtures with reflectors. Automatic timers that will turn the lights on and off on a prescribed growing schedule can be attached to the stands. For the average plant collection, sixteen to eighteen hours of light per day is sufficient.

Persons who are handy with tools may prefer to design and build their own light gardens. Lighting fixtures can be purchased with or without reflectors. If commercial strip fixtures are used, metal reflectors should be made to spread the light over the plants more evenly.

Fluorescent tubes come in various lengths and wattages. There are two-foot (30-watt), three-foot (30-watt), and four-foot (40-watt) tubes. One common formula is 15 to 20 watts of light per foot of growing area measured at the top of the plants. The tubes should be about twelve inches above the pot rims of compact plants, such as those listed on page 171.

Extension offices of agricultural colleges, electric supply stores, and the U.S. Government Printing office supply "how-to" bulletins on construction of light stands. Many botanic gardens give adult courses on gardening under lights. The Indoor Light Gardening Society of America, Inc., is devoted exclusively to growing plants under lights. Membership is open to all interested hobbyists (page 252).

One final reminder when growing plants

A simple single-tube fluorescent lamp fixture and reflector provide enough light for a garden tray and a collection of herb seedlings.

In summer this fireplace is a new focal point with its lighted terrarium.

176

under artificial light: since the light is constant, the plants need regular applications of fertilizer and daily checking for water needs. Daily misting is helpful to keep the humidity high, and grouping potted plants in a tray on a layer of small, moist stones also helps to provide humidity and allows for pot drainage and aeration of roots.

Since plants grown under lights tend to be handled more, lightweight plastic pots and soilless potting mixtures are frequently used rather than clay pots and heavier soil mixes. A simple "recipe" that is popular is a variation of the Cornell mix (page 26). The simplified recipe is one part each of peat moss, vermiculite, and perlite.

indoor gardens

To satisfy that longing to bring the outdoors indoors, more and more homes are including indoor gardens. The ideal type is a sunken garden where plants grow directly in soil at floor level. Since this sort of setup involves rather complicated construction, it should be planned when the house is being built. Putting one in afterward is a costly affair.

Basically, the indoor garden is a "sunken bathtub." A hole or section of the first-floor plan is left open. Concrete blocks, properly sealed to prevent any seepage, are set underneath to shore up the walls of the garden and to confine the planting area. The architect and/or contractor can advise on this important step.

Although the indoor plants will drain into the ground, the bottom of the sunken garden should have drainage gravel at least a foot deep. This will deter plant roots from anchoring deeply into the ground and will provide soil drainage for excess water runoff. The planting area should be filled with good-quality, sterilized planting soil suitable for the types of plants

A sunken garden should be designed and planned before building to insure correct drainage for indoor foliage plants. If designed for a dark area, overhead lighting may be installed.

The ultimate in the indoor garden is an enclosure of the outdoors planned by the architect and interior decorator. Stone house wall, stone steps and outdoor rock blend with a carpet of baby's tears and leafy tropical plants.

to be grown: a rich, loamy type for foliage plants, or a gritty, sandy mixture for cacti and succulents. After the plants are placed, the area can be edged at floor level with interesting stones or lightweight artificial rock for a tidy finish.

A more elegant variation of the sunken garden is the enclosed garden. Again, this is best planned when the house is on the architect's drawing board. Simply, a portion of the outdoors is roofed over, enclosed with glass walls, and left as an open planting space to be enjoyed from the room. This type of indoor garden is more practical in frost-free and mild-winter areas where there would not be the long winter months of central heating. Rocks and stones enhance such a garden for a real "nature indoors" look.

By far the simplest *indoor garden* is a large collection of potted plants arranged in a make-believe "forest" or desert scene in the home. The floor is protected with water-tight metal trays which are filled with pebbles, gravel, wood chips, or sand for outdoor texture. Or you can have a carpenter build a large wooden tray, line it with heavy plastic, and use drainage pebbles. There will be no Mother Earth to plant in, so the plants will have to stay in their individual pots, arranged effectively.

A garden of this dimension indoors just doesn't "happen"; it, too, is preplanned. Those who are clever and knowledgeable about growing plants can design their own garden, but success is more secure if professionals are called in to help. They will have the advantage of experience and may have learned of many pitfalls and techniques unknown to the amateur. These professionals are located in major cities and listed usually as interior garden designers, city gardeners, or home landscapers.

The simplest scheme is to set aside a portion of a room—maybe a living room, den, or dining room—where there is good light from windows, glass walls, or a skylight. Artificial lighting for a large area would be prohibitively expensive and would create too much glare.

Since plants will be grown in individual pots, they can be tended, replaced, or removed easily. Also, there is the dimension of design possibilities with attractive ceramics, tubs, and planters. There are delightful small electrified fountains which can be added for humidity and sound effects.

After the indoor garden room is selected, determine the garden's size. This will be dictated by the dimensions of the room and by how much space can be sacrificed for greenery. The trays can be fashioned in curves, arches, or whatever, but the least expensive will be squares and rectangles. The tinsmith or carpenter should make sure that the trays are watertight and at least 2 inches high (but no higher than 4 to 6 inches). Some tinsmiths and carpenters recommend putting a lath frame or heavy plastic sheeting under the tray to keep it from "sweating" and to allow some aeration. Check this detail out carefully before proceeding.

One reminder: the trays should be filled with attractive drainage material for texture and to catch water runoff when the pots are watered. No water should be allowed to stand in the drainage material as a lazy means of watering. An essential of maintenance for these indoor gardens is that at least once a year they be com-

A large metal tray placed directly on the floor and filled with large pebbles is a dramatic stage for a forest of indoor plants.

184

pletely dismantled and cleaned; drainage material should be washed and rearranged to avoid stale-odor problems and fungi growth.

Plant selection and arrangement is the most fun. The light available will determine what can be grown. Think big, however, and avoid the mistake of selecting many small pots. For a forest of greenery, include enough trees and large-leafed plants to provide a good background. If you want a desert setting, look for some big cacti and natural or artificial rocks. Keep small plants in the front; these can be changed frequently and flowering plants set in for parties and holidays.

Indoor herb gardens are another possibility. The best time to start one is in the spring when many garden centers, florist shops, and even some supermarkets have young herb plants on sale. They are far more rewarding to start with than waiting out the long period necessary for seeds to develop. (The one exception might be basil, which grows quickly from seed.)

The best herbs for growing indoors are basil, parsley, chives, marjoram, mint, sage, savory, and thyme. The other herb plants are just too large for growing in pots. If you have a cool winter room, you can also winter-over rosemary, which normally drops its leaves in a warm room.

Seedling herbs are usually sold in peat pots or plant trays. Repot them in individual clay pots—three- or four-inch size—in a gritty, well-drained soil. (Add some extra sand to the packaged soils sold commercially.) Keep the herbs in a sunny location, especially during the winter months, and water them well, as most of them are thirsty plants. Clipping them frequently for use in cooking will stimulate succulent new growth.

If seedlings cannot be found at garden centers in spring, then plants can be dug from the garden in early fall, or cuttings taken from a neighbor's plants. If all else fails, grow your own seed. Seed packets are available in spring and summer wherever garden supplies are sold.

Where space is limited, but light is good, the plant pole is perfect for a collection of ferns and hanging plants.

office plants

The stark, clean walls of office-building interiors are gently softened by the use of foliage plants. Few places of business are without greenery, which may range from large tubs of tropical foliage trees to wide expanses of planters in lobbies and foyers; from a single pot of pothos on a secretary's desk to a tall tree towering next to the boss's file cabinets.

Plants belong inside office buildings as well as homes, but the choice of what can be grown successfully is limited by special conditions. Most important, and often overlooked, is the shut-down of office ventilating and heating systems when businesses are closed. Temperatures drop, and air circulation ceases. For two or sometimes more days the plants are plunged into a hostile growing environment.

Other hazards are poor lighting, very low humidity, and frequent exposure to drafts from air-conditioning ducts. But even with these disadvantages, foliage plants can live comfortably with computers and typewriters.

189   One of the best ways to decorate with plants

A large wooden planter box planted with dieffenbachia and dracaena makes a strong accent for the formal office.

Banks of large Norfolk Island pine, figs and dracaenas soften the stark walls of office building ground floor space while rows of palms set in trays of white pebbles bring greenery into the offices.

in offices is to utilize a massive arrangement. Large planter tubs filled with an assortment of plants can be dramatic and decorative. They are particularly effective near street level and in reception areas. Groups make a better display than single specimens, and the plants benefit too from air made more humid by mass leaf transpiration.

Among the best plants for offices are Chinese evergreen, *Dracaena*, spathe flower, and ti plant. Where there is strong light, dumb cane and bromeliads might be considered. For very cool offices with good light, a southern yew is a decorative choice.

Where office ceilings are high and a single specimen is desired, an indoor tree is recommended. Among the best indoor trees are the various species of figs (especially *Ficus benjamina* and *F. retusa nitida*), the several large upright philodendrons, two dracaenas *(Dracaena massangeana* and *D. marginata),* and the Swiss cheese plant. Vines that grow well are kangaroo vine, several philodendrons, and pothos.

bottle gardens and terrariums

A bottle garden is a miniature landscape growing in a glass container which can be practically whatever imagination dictates—a fish bowl, a large brandy snifter, a five-gallon jug, an antique bottle of clear (not colored) glass, or even some of the contemporary plastic boxes. Inside the container the plants function in their own little ecosystem which is self-maintaining. A terrarium is a bottle garden, too, but the name more correctly applies to a collection of woodland wild plants.

Since the containers for these gardens are limited in space with small openings, small-sized plants are used for planting. Also, there is less chance that they will be damaged in handling if they are small. The best plants to use are small, rooted cuttings, or seedlings of house plants. Good choices are ferns, *Fittonia*, ivies, or baby's tears for ground cover, small-leaved fig, begonias, young palms, dracaenas, peperomias, and the like.

When selecting plants, strive for an interesting assortment of pattern and shape. Combine

A triangular shaped terrarium houses dracaena, pothos and holly fern.

colored foliage plants, variegated plants, arrow-shaped leaves, round leaves, and flat-leaved plants, with heights ranging from tall, to short, to ground cover. These young plants may be difficult to find, but large-scale greenhouses that do their own propagating can usually supply them. Or some mail-order houses can. If there is time, cuttings can be rooted from your house-plant collection, or seeds can be started.

Wild plants for terrariums are quite often on state conservation lists and not to be dug up. If you have your own woodlands or access to the woods of a friend you are indeed fortunate. Do this in early autumn, just before the leaves fall. Lacking your own woods, young wild plants can be purchased from mail-order wildflower nurseries. Some of the best plants for the woodland terrarium are mosses for groundcover, partridgeberry, pipsissewa, rattlesnake plantain, seedlings of pines, spruces, and other woodland conifers, almost all of the woodland ferns, and ground pine. And for the finishing touches, small rocks and pieces of wood or bark on which lichens are growing are real treasures.

Planting of these gardens is a bit tricky as the quarters are cramped. If the container is an aquarium or wide-mouthed jar or bottle, the task is much simpler. More challenging are the narrow-necked bottles. In any case, the rules are the same. The first layer inside the bottle or terrarium should be a good drainage layer, either coarse builder's sand or very fine gravel. If it is more convenient, buy bird gravel in pet stores or dime stores, a mixture of fine gravel, oyster shells, and clay. The depth of the drainage layer is in proportion to the size and design of the container. Its purpose is to serve as a

A five-gallon water jug is a challenge to plant but rewarding. The self-maintaining garden will last for many years.

196

A modification of the demijohn has an opening so that it can be planted and tended easily as a bottle garden.

The plastic terrarium, without the old-fashioned metal supports, is ideal for a larger selection of plants.

The five-gallon water jug is available with an opening tor gardeners who find the narrow open top too difficult.

catch-all for excess water.

Next comes the soil mixture. Since the plants are going to stay put for quite some time, the soil mixture should be rich and well blended with humus. The general "recipe"—one part sand, one part humus, and one part sterilized soil—is a good basic one, with perhaps a little extra humus added and some bone meal, too. For narrow-necked bottles, use either a plastic food funnel or long cardboard tube to insert the soil.

Next, the plants themselves, one by one. Long wooden tongs are ideal for handling plants. Hold each plant between the tongs and insert it inside the container. If you can get your hands or a few fingers inside to tuck in the roots, the job is much simpler.

Arrange the plants in a banked effect, piling the soil higher in the back and lower toward the front. Put tall plants in the back, the lower plants toward the front and sides, and ground covers at the base.

After the plants are in place, sift a little extra soil in and around them to be sure all the tiny roots are covered. Then, with a mister, spray the foliage and then mist the soil until thoroughly wet. (You can see the soil becoming darker as the water is absorbed.) Mist the sides of the glass to wash down any soil that spilled. Then put on the glass top or cork the bottle and the garden is on its own. Keep it out of strong light for a few days until the plants adjust to their new surroundings.

Once the garden is settled, it cares for itself fairly well. The tiny ecosystem replenishes its own moisture through transpiration and manufactures its own oxygen. If too much moisture

If too much moisture condenses on the insides of a bottle garden, as shown at the left, remove the top for a few hours until it clears.

condenses on the sides and lid, take the top off for a few hours. Controlling excess moisture is the chief problem with bottle gardens and terrariums. Once the little ecosystem cycle gets going, however, there should be no problem, and many of these bottle gardens have been known to last for several years. Occasionally, it may be necessary to prune out a dead leaf or replace a dead or overgrown plant. (Being confined, they usually grow very slowly.) But the gardens really do seem to grow on and on forever. Keep them in bright light, possibly direct sunlight during the winter months.

Bottle gardens and terrariums have also proved successful with fluorescent light. For this, gesneriads, such as tiny, inch-high gloxinias, and some of the rare miniature house plants that require high humidity are excellent choices. For sources of such plants, see p. 254.

hanging plants

What could be prettier than a lipstick vine in full bloom hanging from a handsome wall bracket? Decorative containers with trailing plants are catching on as an imaginative way to grow plants. Many hobbyists who once thought they didn't have any more space for plants, now find that hanging them is the perfect solution.

Hanging planters ready to be filled with plants are available at garden centers, pottery shops, specialty houses, and florist shops. Or planters filled with plants may be purchased and hung immediately. Most of the newer ones have some kind of drainage saucer built in to catch any overflow from watering. The large, old-fashioned basket types, lined with sphagnum moss and then filled with soil, are better for use outdoors since they drip after watering. The most interesting planters are handcrafted pots of glazed or unglazed clay. There are also planters of brass and copper. Less expensive are pottery or plastic pots with holes bored in their rims for hanging. Handwoven baskets are becoming popular, but be sure to use plastic liners

Fuchsias are one of the showiest plants for hanging.

or buy them large enough to put a drainage pot or saucer inside. For contemporary decor there are plastic bowls with holes bored in their rims for hanging.

Planters are hung with whatever strikes the fancy—chains, nylon ropes, leather thongs, strong wire, or metal clips. Wall brackets, side hooks, or ceiling hooks are used for attachment. Various other decorative hangers can also be devised. The most important thing about the support is that it should be fixed securely to the wall or ceiling. Heavy clay planters are even heavier when the soil is wet. Strong fasteners, such as molly bolts or toggles, should be used. Also, wall brackets should extend far enough from walls to give the plants room to branch and spread out without being cramped or lop-sided.

As to what to grow, the choices are ever expanding. The amount of light available will be the determining factor. Where there is good bright light—an east or west window—flowering plants are ideal. Southern windows are good for flowering plants, provided the hanging plants are shielded from strong sun. They can be vacationed outdoors in summer, hung from the patio or a roof overhang. Where the light is less strong, nonflowering foliage plants are the best choice. The following lists suggest some possibilities:

for flowers

Begonia	Ivy geranium
Campanula isophylla	Jasmine
Christmas cactus	*Lantana*
Episcia	Lipstick vine
Fuchsia	*Oxalis*
Hoya	String of hearts

for foliage

Asparagus fern	Piggyback plant
Chlorophytum	Pothos
Cissus	Rhipsalis
Ferns	Saxifraga
Ivies	Swedish ivy
Lamium	Tradescantia
Philodendron	Velvet plant
	Zebrina

The procedure for planting hanging plants is the same as for pot plants. Place a piece of crock or shard over the drainage hole, and add a small amount of drainage material. Partly fill the container with a fibrous potting mixture, enriched with compost or peat moss. (This enables the soil to hold moisture well.) Then set the plant or plants in the container. With large hanging-basket pottery or the oval dish type, three plants may be needed to fill it attractively. Arrange them so that the vines hang gracefully, then fill in with soil and water well. Drain at the sink until it stops dripping.

Upkeep of hanging plants is not much different than most house plants, with possibly two exceptions: during the winter months, when heat indoors rises and humidity goes down, the hanging planters may dry out more quickly than one might suspect. Check them every few days. It will take a bit of practice to know if the planter is well soaked. Until watering is perfected, take the planters down and water them at the sink, making a mental note of the amount of water needed. After a few trials, you will know how much water to provide each time. With planters that have built-in saucers, water as you would any potted plant—that is, until water appears in the saucer below.

A brass planter makes an attractive hanging planter for this wandering jew.

A well-grown spider plant highlights a plant collection. Ceiling hangers must be installed solidly to support the considerable weight of the plant.

Staghorn ferns attached to wood plaques thrive in a moist indoor climate.

Another point to remember is to hang plants in prominent positions. They look their best when they are hung at just eye level or above. Give them frequent inspections; pull off any dead leaves, prune them back if necessary to keep them shapely, and turn them every few weeks so that all sides get their share of light. A shower bath at the sink once every few weeks is a good practice to follow.

Feed these plants the same way you would any pot plants—regular feeding when the plants are growing well during the spring, summer, and early fall months, less feeding during the dormant winter months. Any standard house-plant fertilizer used according to directions is fine. Most hanging planters should last for twelve to eighteen months without repotting, but if a plant shows signs of waning growth, yellowing leaves, and lack of bloom, it may be root bound and need repotting or thinning.

Another idea for hanging plants are the dramatic staghorn ferns. The unusual fertile fronds look like deer or elk antlers, while the flat, barren fronds support the "antlers" and shield the anchoring roots. This fern is an epiphyte or air plant and grows on tropical trees in Africa, Malaya, Java and Madagascar. As a house fern, the plant grows very well with little care. Mist it every few days, water when the root fiber feels dry to the touch and keep it in a cool, bright place, away from direct sunlight.

These ferns can be purchased on decorative wood hanging plaques from quality greenhouse growers and well-stocked plant shops. Or, if you have an interesting piece of cork bark or driftwood, you might like to "plant" your own. The fern is self-anchoring, once the tiny threadlike

Queen's tears, a bromeliad, makes a delightful hanging basket.

roots have grown into the rooting fiber. To make a place for the roots to take hold, gouge out a wide deep hole into the bark or driftwood and pack it well with thoroughly wetted orchid potting fiber or sphagnum moss. If the fiber or moss does not pack in firmly, it may be necessary to tie it down with fish line which will be cut away when the fern is well rooted into the rooting medium and bark. Then place the staghorn fern over the area where the rooting medium is packed. A large fern should be secured with wooden florist picks. Lay the fern and support flat on a table, and mist it daily until you are sure the roots have anchored in well. This may take several days or weeks depending on the size of the fern. When rooted and securely held, the staghorn fern is ready for hanging where it will show to advantage. If properly cared for, it will last for many years.

topiary

Topiary is the art of training plants to special forms. The Romans were known for their beautifully "carved" boxwood, and during the Renaissance, this art flourished in the gardens of Italy and France. Many examples of the art of topiary survive today to inspire modern interpretations. To translate this technique of pruning and clipping to house-plant scale is indeed a challenge, but rewarding if met!

There are two ways of achieving house-plant topiary: by stuffing ready-made wire forms with sphagnum moss and planting low growing plants over its surface, or by training plants on a metal frame which supports them as they grow.

The stuffing method utilizes a form shaped like a dog, rabbit, turtle, squirrel, or other animal, or a geometric form such as a cone, globe, or triangle. Though forms are available commercially, the more ambitious may want to shape their own out of chicken wire and No. 8 or 10 galvanized wire. The basic frame of the body shape is made of a cylinder of chicken wire squashed in and rounded where needed to con-

A fluffy poodle, made of ivy plants, requires high humidity to flourish. Daily misting greatly aids maintenance.

The owl frame and newly begun lollipop topiary are both good forms for beginners.

The candelabra and heart make delightful topiary accents when covered with ivy, hoya, clematis or other vines.

form to the desired shape. If an animal, the head, legs, and tail are fashioned with wire spirals and fastened to the chicken-wire frame.

Once the shape is made, the core of the body is stuffed with sphagnum moss that has been soaking in a bucket of water. Squeeze it out well and poke it in tightly with a long stick. Handfuls of the moss are wrapped around the "limbs" of the animal shapes and secured with cotton-covered rust-proof wire.

Now the topiary form is ready for its finishing coat of greenery. Rooted cuttings of ivy—the small-leaved types such as needlepoint or shamrock—are used. These varieties grow flat and are well suited to topiary. Tuck the root ends of the cuttings deep into the moss and pin them down firmly with pieces of cotton-covered wire cut and bent like hairpins. (Real hairpins will rust.) Patience is required for the topiary will not look elegant and lusciously green for some time, possibly a year to eighteen months. Mist the ivy at least once a day, keep the form in a cool, bright but not sunny place, and feed by spraying the leaves every two to three weeks with a water-soluble plant food. This method where the nutrients are absorbed by the leaves is called foliar feeding.

As the ivy grows, pin down the long strands to conform to the shape, and prune back those that are unwieldy. During the summer months, the ivy topiary can be kept outdoors. In winter, bring it back inside, either to a cool greenhouse or a cool room where there is good light. The topiary will go through a somewhat dormant state, but it will come back with misting and care. For those who have mastered working with ivy, creeping fig is another good choice.

A well-grown topiary circle requires several years to fill in properly and reach its optimum beauty.

The other type of topiary—equally challenging—involves training long strands of pot-grown vines over and around a metal frame. For this, there is a wider choice of plants. Almost any type of vine, such as ivy, *Cissus, Hoya, Clematis,* and creeping fig, can be used. A simple shape is best for learning, such as a lattice, heart shape, oval, or globe on a pole or a fan. Most of the forms are on weighted supports so they will not be top-heavy. Stand the weighted form in the bottom of a clay pot, four or five inches in diameter. Add soil, then set in the plant—preferably one that has a few long strands—and firm it well into the soil mixture. To start the ivy, or whatever plant is chosen, on its training upward and around the form, cotton-covered wire is used to fasten the plant loosely to the frame. Do not hesitate to clip and shape where needed, always using a sharp pruning shears. Like the stuffed topiary, daily misting and a regular feeding program are necessary to keep the plants growing along rapidly. These topiaries can also go outside during the summer months and are wintered in a cool bright room or greenhouse.

standards

The tubbed orange trees in the seventeenth-century French gardens may have inspired the shapes of modern-day standard plants. The orange trees, tender in some of the European climates, were grown in huge wooden boxes which were rolled outdoors during the mild summer weather and rolled back into protective greenhouses for the winter months. They were clipped and shaped so that their size was in pleasing proportion to the box, with the result that they resembled so many boxed "lollipops." This form may have inspired the tree roses, tree geraniums, tree lantanas, etc., grown today. Professionals call plants trained in this manner "standards."

Most standards are expensive to buy since intensive training and maintenance have gone into them. With a little guidance and practice, however, these plants can be trained at home. Favorite choices to train are fuchsias, lantanas, geraniums, and, when the technique is perfected, woody herbs as rosemary or lavender. Shrubs, particularly forsythia, will train easily.

222

One of the simplest plants for beginners to start with is lantana, as follows: in spring, buy a strong, erect plant. If it is not growing in what appears to be a good, fertile, soil mixture, repot it in a four- or five-inch clay pot. Select a single stem that will provide the straightest, strongest support. Clip off all other branches with a sharp clipper to avoid tearing the bark. Choose a tall, sturdy, plant stake, three to four feet tall, and poke it down into the pot, near the stem.

The "whip," as the plant is now called, is pushed along to grow rapidly. Feed it regularly with any house-plant fertilizer, and keep it indoors in a warm, sunny site. As the whip grows, rub off any side buds that start to develop with your thumb. The goal is a long, straight, woody stem. Tie it loosely to the stake to keep it upright. It may take two to three months for the whip to be tall enough for top training, about three to four feet high.

When the whip has reached the height desired, stop the upward growth by topping the plant; that is, clip out the terminal bud to the first leaf axil. This will force the plant to send out many side branches at the top. As these develop, keep clipping back each branch to two rows of leaves. This continues until the plant begins to develop a well-rounded head on top of a straight, sturdy, branchless stem. From start to finish, the training may require two full years.

The fully-trained standard can be kept outdoors all summer. During the winter months, keep it indoors and cut the rounded top back hard, to three- to five-inch stubs. Place the standard in a cool place and water sparingly to induce a semidormant state until early spring.

forcing bulbs

W inter can be a drab season for house-plant growers because the sun is softer in the sky and so many of the plants go through a semidormant period. This is a scene where some bulb flowers can do some brightening. Hardy bulbs—that is, bulbs that endure cold temperatures—are planted in gardens in the fall to bloom outdoors in spring. When these same hardy bulbs are planted in pots and encouraged to root and blossom in January, February, or March, not their normal flowering season, this is called "forcing." Florists have been forcing bulbs for years for gift sales at Eastertime, and more recently for Valentine's Day and Mother's Day. Now more home folks are mastering the method and are forcing bulbs with great success.

There are many kinds of hardy bulbs to force. The big three—daffodils, tulips, and hyacinths—are the favorites, but more charming are the little bulbs—*Crocus, Scilla,* and bulbous iris.

Not all varieties of hardy bulbs adapt well to forcing. Bulb growers list the best forcing varieties in their catalogs, and garden centers and retail outlets will also supply this information. Plan the number of pots you want to fill with bulbs and make a shopping list before venturing forth in October.

Hyacinths look best one to a four-inch pot. Tulips, usually the lower-growing cottage, single early, and doubles, should be potted several to a pot, as should daffodils. Clay pans, if available, are better suited to bulb forcing, since they are shorter than pots and the roots grow best in the shallower depth. They come in several sizes; six-inch pans can accommodate six to eight tulip bulbs or three to four of the large-sized daffodil bulbs. The little bulbs look best in a four- or five-inch pan.

For soil, packaged potting soil is fine. The soil serves mostly as an anchor for the bulb's root system; the flowers and leaves were already formed when the bulbs were dug from the growing fields.

When potting, fill the pot about halfway with soil. Gauge soil level so that the tips of the bulbs will be just below the top of the soil. Firm the first layer of soil down, then arrange the bulbs pointed end up on top of it and fill in around them with the rest of the soil. Water thoroughly. Sometimes the simplest way is to water from the bottom by putting the pans or pots in large trays of water and allowing the water to soak up through the drainage holes until the soil appears wet. Remove and drain.

Store the potted bulbs in a cool, dark place, for now the bulbs must develop a root system. A garage, basement, or unheated room is a good place. The pots should stay there for at least a month or six weeks to be sure there is good root development. By this time it is De-

Seven crocus corms will fit nicely into a five-inch pot.

226

cember and outdoor temperatures will be colder. The next step is cold storage. Either pack the bulb pans and pots into a coldframe and cover them well with straw, hay, or leaf mulch, or pack them into large cartons filled with straw and the like and cover them well. This method is good for city penthouse gardeners. The object is to keep the bulbs cold, but not permit them to freeze.

One by one, starting in late January or early February, the pots or pans can be brought indoors to force the bulbs into flowering. Introduce them to gradually warmer temperatures. The leaves must grow first, so keep the pots in a cool but not too bright place. After foliage begins to develop, gradually move the plants to warmer temperatures and stronger light. Once the leaf growth is under way, the bulbs can be grown in fairly full sunlight until the flower buds begin to fill out. When flower buds open, moving the plants to a cooler place will help the blossoms last longer. During this forcing, be sure the soil is moist at all times.

Once the bulbs have been forced, most gardeners toss the bulbs away. If you choose they can be grown in pots to keep the foliage green. When the leaves yellow, store the pots in an out-of-the-way place. When fall bulb-planting time comes around, plant them. They will not amount to much of anything for several years as forcing takes its toll.

Those who live in warm climates have some success in forcing hardy bulbs by storing them in the back of the refrigerator for a month or so. Then the bulbs are potted, kept moist to initiate root growth, and forced right along to flowering. Since they have already had their "cool" period, there is no need to chill them further.

fun for children

Youngsters love to watch things grow. To start this learning at an early age will reap rich dividends for future years. Plant growing teaches children awareness and observation, and affords early lessons in responsibility, for an untended plant too soon collapses.

When to start? Three- and four-year-olds learn to appreciate how things grow, although most mothers will find more attentive beginners at ages five to seven. By the time a youngster reaches his teens group activities will usually occupy him and interest in plants may wane.

What to grow? A favorite first plant with most children is a pretty plant, one with flowers. An African violet or a begonia can be very special. If the learning begins during the winter months, a paperwhite *Narcissus* is a fast-developing plant that will thrill young eyes as the long leaves grow and the flower stalk appears.

From the pretty plants, youngsters graduate to seeds, the kinds of seeds that develop quickly or at least show some early signs of doing something. The youngest gardeners lose patience if

Children can enjoy the responsibilities attendant in caring for plants.

anything takes more than a few days for action. Some of the kitchen plants—pineapple tops, carrot tops, sweet potatoes, bean seeds, lentils, citrus-fruit seeds, etc.—are fun projects for them.

A few pointers on getting started. The plant should have a special place in the child's home or apartment, either in his bedroom or on a sunny, bright shelf where the youngster can easily reach and tend it. If there are younger brothers or sisters around, be sure to keep the plant out of harm's way.

Watchful guidance and perhaps a few reminders on care (and checking by mother or dad) for the first few weeks are usually necessary to get the routine going. It helps, too, if someone else is "caring about the plant." Gradually, full responsibility should fall on the youngster's shoulders.

The container is not too important. Try sawed-in-half quart milk cartons with a few holes poked in the bottom with an ice pick for drainage. Or try clay pots. The plastic pots usually do not dry out as quickly and youngsters have a tendency to overwater. Any of the packaged potting mixtures sold in dime stores, garden shops, and hardware stores are fine to use.

Following are a few special pointers on specific plants for children:

annuals Small-growing plants such as marigolds and alyssum bloom bountifully on a winter windowsill. Use packaged potting soil, and purchase seed in summer for winter projects. Seed packets are not available in the winter months.

avocado Select a ripe avocado and remove the

pit carefully. Wash the pit thoroughly and dry it. The pit may be suspended over a glass of water so that just the bottom touches the water, held there by three toothpicks pressed firmly into the sides. Or else the pit may be potted directly in the soil (the broad base is the bottom) with about one-fourth of the pit protruding from the soil. Either method may take several weeks for signs of growth. With the water-glass method, pot the avocado as soon as the root develops. The avocado will grow into a long telephone-pole plant unless the growing tip is pinched out as soon as the stem attains several inches of growth. This forces the plant to branch. The plant will not attain fruiting size indoors. (Mature avocado trees are about the size of an apple tree.) It is a good idea to start two or three pits at once as only a fully mature avocado pit will develop roots. It is impossible to know from their appearance which avocados are the desirable mature ones when you buy them in the store. The best insurance against a dud is starting several at once.

carrot Cut one-half inch off the top of the carrot and place it in damp sand. Keep it damp and in strong light. Very soon lovely foliage will start to appear. The foliage will eventually spend itself out, and children should not expect to harvest carrots from the plant. The top is grown just "for pretty." Beets and turnips can be grown the same way.

coffee Seeds of *unroasted* coffee beans, if you can find them, can be grown into handsome, waxy-leaved house plants. They need warm sunlight to succeed and should not be exposed to drafts.

citrus Seeds of all the breakfast fruits—oranges, grapefruit, or even lemons—are easy to plant and grow. Select large seeds, wash and dry them. Plant several to a pot. If they all germinate, cut off the weakest with scissors and allow only one to grow per pot. Keep the seedlings in a warm sunny site. All the citrus plants have attractive, shiny leaves, but these plants should not be expected to bear fruit. However, the dwarf, ornamental citrus will bear fruit and is widely available wherever house plants are sold.

coleus This delightful colored foliage plant grows easily from seed. One packet will supply an entire classroom with individual plants. Again, buy seed in summer; it will not be available in winter. The sunnier the growing place, the brighter the coleus foliage colors will be. This plant needs frequent pruning back to keep it from becoming tall and spindly.

dates Unpasteurized dates (usually available in health-food stores) are the source of date pits for planting. Pits from pasteurized dates will not germinate. Plant the pits in a sandy soil, several seeds to a pot to be sure at least one sprouts. Then grow the palm in a bright, sunny window.

grapes Seeds from grapes are fun to plant and will grow aggressively into a vine. One large pot about four or five inches can support two or three seedlings. Grow the grapevines near a window or a trellis of some kind so the vines can be trained around it.

lentils Place lentils in a shallow dish of sand, kept moist, and the lentils will sprout into lovely fresh greens which will last for several weeks.

Paperwhite narcissus bulbs are inexpensive, quick to grow and rewarding for youngsters.

234

paperwhite narcissus These tender bulbs appear in dime stores and garden centers during the winter months. They are inexpensive, so buy several. Plant them in shallow dishes or bowls, several to a dish, filled with pebbles or marble chips. Place the bulbs halfway in the pebbles with their top halves exposed. Keep water just to the bottom of the bulbs and place the dish in a dark place for ten days or so until roots form. Then bring the dish to bright light to encourage the leaves to push up. Gradually bring to full sunlight to bring on the sweetly fragrant flowers. Once the flowers fade, the bulbs are discarded.

sensitive plant This is a fascinating plant for children. The leaves respond to touch or heat and fold up. Seed is available in packets at gardening centers. Follow package directions.

sweet potato If untreated sweet potatoes can be found, try growing one. (Most commercially available potatoes and sweet potatoes are pretreated to prevent bud sprouting.) Place the sweet potato uncut in a large vase or jar of water so just the bottom touches the water and place it in a bright warm place. Soon the sprouts will begin to emerge, and eventually leaves and vinelike growth. The sweet potato can continue to be grown in water or may be potted.

pineapple top Sever the top from a fully ripened pineapple so that just a small, flat piece of the fruit is attached to the leaves—enough to hold on to. Pull off the bottom leaves and allow the top to dry for a day. Then anchor it in a shallow bowl of pebbles or sandy soil and keep it damp. Mist the foliage frequently. Eventually roots will form and new growth will appear on top. If bottom leaves yellow, pull them out.

vegetables Though they will not be plentiful enough for a family salad, radishes and leaf lettuce are fun for tots to grow. Plant the seed in large pots and grow them in a sunny window. Radishes are quick to grow—three weeks from seed to harvest.

The following plants are, for various reasons, generally not successful with children.

cactus They take too long to do anything and are boring for children to grow.

vines Ivy, *Hoya, Cissus,* etc., are slow-growing and not very exciting to watch develop.

outdoor plants Hardy trees and shrub seedlings are not house plants as they require the cycle of the seasons to be successful.

propagation

There are many ways to increase the number of indoor plants by propagation. The simplest ways are by rooting stem or leaf cuttings, rooting runners, planting seeds, and air layering.

rooting stem cuttings *Begonia,* geranium, and most other house plants that grow upright with long stems can be propagated by snipping off and planting sections of the stem. These pieces of the plant are called cuttings, or slips, as grandmothers might say. Select vigorous, upright-growing shoots, several inches long, with four to six leaves, and sever the shoots from the plant with a sharp knife.

The rooting medium can be bought or mixed at home. Vermiculite or perlite, two substances that hold moisture well, are available in dime stores, garden centers, and hardware stores in packages of varying quantity. Both are excellent for rooting cuttings. A homemade mixture that many commercial propagators still use is a half-perlite and half-peat-moss mixture.

A plastic or clay pot can be used for just a few

cuttings. Fill it almost to the top with the rooting medium and water it thoroughly. While it drains, trim the bottom leaves off the cuttings. Using a pencil, poke a hole in the rooting medium and insert the cutting. Space cuttings without crowding. Then water again to settle the rooting medium around the cuttings and to eliminate any air pockets. Drain, then cover the pot by slipping a plastic freezer bag over the top and securing it around the pot rim with a rubber band. Place the cuttings in bright light, but not direct sun.

For rooting a greater number of cuttings, a transparent plastic box with a lid works best, such as a bread box or vegetable refrigerator box. Poke a few holes in the bottom of the box with a red-hot ice pick or other sharp instrument (heated in the gas-stove flame) to permit excess water to drain out. Fill the box about one-third full with the rooting medium. This will allow space for the cuttings to stand upright when the lid is closed. Again, water first and drain; trim the lower leaves and insert cuttings in medium; water again, and put on the lid. Keep out of direct sun.

Check the cuttings in about ten days to see if roots are forming. Tug gently on a cutting. If it resists, roots are probably well formed. If no roots have formed and the cutting pulls out, tuck it back in and wait a while longer.

Sections taken from the long "woody" stems of plants such as *Dracaena*, dumb cane, and ti plant will root if placed in damp sand or sphagnum moss. Cut pieces several inches long, set them on their sides, and press them down into the rooting medium so just a tiny portion of the bark shows. In several weeks, the eyes, undevel-

Remove geranium cuttings from young stems of a plant with a sharp knife. After trimming off bottom leaves, put cuttings into a pot filled with rooting medium and keep out of direct sunlight until the cuttings are rooted.

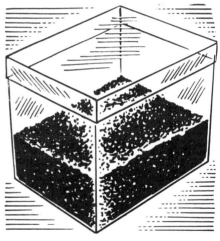

A clay pot filled with growing medium and covered with a plastic refrigerator bag, or a plastic food dish filled with growing medium, can be used for propagating plants. Poke holes in the plastic dish for drainage with a hot ice pick.

oped buds which look like bumps on the stem, will sprout roots and new plants. These may be potted and grown individually.

rooting leaf cuttings African violets can be rooted from leaves. Each leaf must have a half-inch of the leaf stem, or petiole, attached to it when it is removed from the plant. Insert the stem end of the leaf in a rooting medium (see *Rooting stem cuttings*) that has been moistened. After roots form, in about four weeks, small plantlets will start to grow at the base of each leaf. Sometimes plantlets take about two months to form, so be patient. Sever each new plant from the mother leaf and pot separately.

Many hobbyists are successful in rooting African violet leaves in water. Use a rubber band to secure a piece of waxed paper over the top of a small glass filled with water. Poke a small hole in the paper and insert the petiole in the water. Keep the glass in bright light.

Two-inch-long pieces of snake-plant leaves cut across the width of the leaf and inserted upright in a growing medium will also root if kept in a cool moist place.

A *rex Begonia* leaf will root if it is placed flat on top of a sand and peat-moss mixture kept moist and out of direct sun. Pin it down at the veins with small hairpins to keep the leaf in contact with the soil. Make a few cuts at the main veins where little plants will form. Wedge-shaped cuttings can be made from the leaf; each should have a section of the main vein plus a small section of the leaf stem (petiole) attached.

rooting runners Many plants increase naturally by putting out runners from their bases. The most popular house plants that do this are flame violet, spider plant, and strawberry geranium. Small plantlets form at the tips of long runners. These are easy to root, simply by pinning them down in the soil of the pot until they develop roots. Then the plantlets can be severed from the mother plant, dug up, and potted individually.

Or put small satellite pots filled with a sandy soil mixture around the base of the plant and pin a plantlet down to the surface of each. When plantlets are rooted, simply sever them from the mother plant and grow them individually.

planting seeds   Starting a plant from a seed is a bit more specialized than rooting cuttings or runners. Yet, it is one way of getting some of the more unusual types of plants and is more of a challenge to the hobbyist. Seeds of common house plants are obtained from seed racks and seed catalogs (page 255). Rare seeds of unusual house plants are usually available through seed exchanges between members of various plant societies (page 251).

Seed requires an incubation period to germinate. For this reason, it is practical to start them in covered transparent containers, such as small plastic refrigerator dishes, laboratory petri dishes, and small glass jars. Milled sphagnum moss is the best starting medium, or "starter" mix can be purchased prepackaged at the dime store. Both are sterile, which eliminates the problem of "damping off," a fungus disease that often fells young seedlings. Milled sphagnum moss is available commercially, but if it cannot be found, buy unmilled sphagnum moss and

An African violet leaf can be rooted by inserting the stem into a glass of water and collaring it with a piece of wax paper tied in place. Roots form at the base of the leaf and the plantlet is then potted. The mother leaf is cut off.

The spider plant is easy to propagate by placing satellite pots filled with soil around the base of the mother plant. Attach the tiny runner plants to the soil with a surface toothpick and sever runner from the stem when plantlet is well rooted.

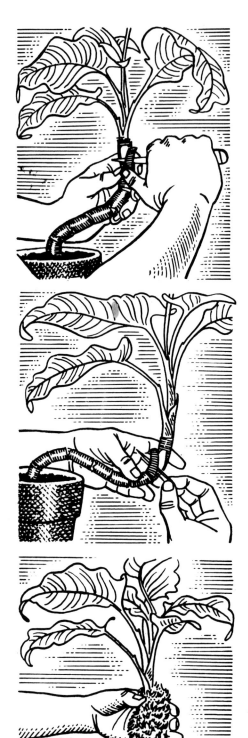

Air layering is one way to solve the problem of a dieffenbachia (or similar plant) that has outgrown its pot and become too tall or mis-shapen. Make a slanting cut part way through the stem and insert a piece of toothpick. Wrap damp sphagnum moss around the cut.

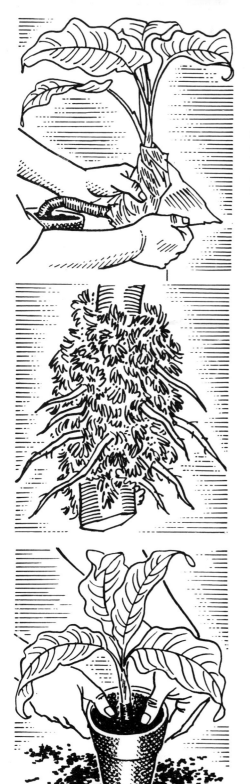

Cover with plastic tied on the top and bottom. Roots will form in several weeks. Then cut off the plant and pot it. The mother plant should not be discarded as it will also resprout.

rub it through a wire screen.

Moisten the moss thoroughly with warm water before planting the seed. (Do this carefully, since the moss is fluffy, like powder.) When the moss is wet, allow it to drain well and then plant the seed. Since most house-plant seed is very fine, it is generally just sprinkled lightly on top of the moist moss. It gradually works its way down into the medium.

If possible, don't remove the lid of a seed container until germination has taken place. Keep the container in a heavily shaded corner where it won't be disturbed by pets and children. The first pair of leaves to appear are not usually true leaves, but serve to nourish the seedling and the true leaves to come. The second pair are *true* leaves. After a second pair forms, the seedlings may be transplanted to a growing medium and given the same care as other house plants.

air layering This form of propagation causes roots to form on a stem, which is then severed from the mother plant and grown separately. It is an excellent solution for cutting down to size the house plant that has grown too tall, plants such as *Ficus, Dieffenbachia, Dracaena,* etc. Several air layers can be made on multistemmed plants at the same time.

To air layer a *Ficus, Dieffenbachia,* or *Dracaena,* make a cut halfway through the main stem about one-third down from the growing tip. Insert a small piece of toothpick to keep the cut slightly open. Then wrap thoroughly dampened sphagnum moss around the cut area. Tie a piece of plastic sheeting around the moss and make it airtight by securing it above and below with string. **Care** for the plant normally. **Roots** will form inside the ball of moss in several weeks to several months, depending on the species of plant and the environment. When roots are visible through the plastic, sever the "plantlet" from the mother plant just below the plastic wrapping, pot it, and for a few days keep it covered with a plastic bag to give the roots time to establish themselves. Now you have two plants—the newly rooted top and the mother-plant base which will resprout if cared for normally.

house plant societies

The African Violet Society of America, Inc.
Box 1326
Knoxville, Tenn. 37901

American Begonia Society
1431 Coronado Terrace
Los Angeles, Calif. 90026

The American Fuchsia Society
Mrs. Lillian Lee, Sec.
738 - 22nd Avenue
San Francisco, Calif. 94121

The American Gesneria Society
Mr. Edgar Sherer
11983 Darlington Avenue
Los Angeles, Calif. 90049

The American Gloxinia and Gesneriad Society, Inc.
Mrs. Diantha Buell, Sec.
Eastford, Conn. 06242

The American Orchid Society, Inc.
Botanical Museum of Harvard University
Cambridge, Mass. 02138

Bromeliad Society
Mrs. Jeanne Woodbury
1811 Edgecliff Drive
Los Angeles, Calif. 90026

Cactus and Succulent Society of America, Inc.

Box 167
Reseda, Calif. 91335

The Indoor Light Gardening Society of America, Inc.

Mrs. James Martin, Membership Secretary
1316 Warren Road
Lakewood, Ohio 44107

International Geranium Society

1413 Shoreline Road
Santa Barbara, Calif. 93105

Saintpaulia International

Box 10604
Knoxville, Tenn. 37919

where to get plants and supplies

african violets

Fischer Greenhouses
Linwood, N.J.   08221

Tinari Greenhouses
2325 Valley Road
Huntingdon Valley, Pa.   19006

begonias

Logee's Greenhouses
55 North Street
Danielson, Conn.   06239

foliage plants

Alberts & Merkel Bros., Inc.
P.O. Box 637
Boynton Beach, Fla.   33435

Nielsen's Florist and Garden Center (no mail order)
1405 Post Road
Darien, Conn.   06820

cacti and succulents

Ben Haines
1902 Lane
Topeka, Kansas   66604

Davis Cactus Garden
Kerrville, Texas   78028

Henrietta's Nursery
1345 N. Brawley Avenue
Fresno, Calif.   93705

geraniums

Cook's Geranium Nursery
Lyons, Kansas 67554

Merry Gardens
Camden, Maine 04843

Wilson Brothers
Roachdale, Ind. 46172

gesneriads *(African violets, Brazilian edelweiss, columnea, flame violet, gloxinia, kohleria, lipstick plant, nautilocalyx, sinningia, streptocarpus and temple bells.)*

Buell's Greenhouses
Eastford, Conn. 06242

Lyndon Lyon
14 Mutchler Street
Dolgeville, N.Y. 13329

Tropical Paradise Greenhouses
8825 W. 79th Street
Overland Park, Kansas 66200

Kartuz Greenhouses
92 Chestnut Street
Wilmington, Mass. 01887

orchids

McClellan Co.
1450 El Camino Real
South San Francisco, Calif. 94080

Margaret Ilgenfritz
Monroe, Mich. 48161

Lager & Hurrell
426 Morris Avenue
Summit, N.J. 07901

wildflowers for terrariums

Mincemoyers
R.D. 5
Jackson, N.J. 08527

Putney Nursery, Inc.
Putney, Vermont 05346

Vick's Wildgardens, Inc.
Box 115
Gladwyne, Pa. 19035

SUPPLIES

seeds

Burgess Seed and Plant Co.
Galesburg, Mich.   49053

W. Atlee Burpee Co.
Philadelphia, Pa.   19132

Henry Field Seed and Nursery Co.
Shenandoah, Iowa   51601

George W. Park Seed Co.
Greenwood, S.C.   29646

bulbs

Antonelli Bros.
2545 Capitola Road
Santa Cruz, Calif.   95060

DeJager and Sons, Inc.
South Hamilton, Mass.   01982

J. Howard French
Baltimore Pike
Lima, Pa.   19060

Oakhurst Gardens
345 W. Colorado Street
Arcadia, Calif.   91006

John Scheepers, Inc.
63 Wall Street
New York, N.Y.   10005

fertilizers

Hydroponic Chemical Co.
Copley, Ohio   44321

Robert B. Peters Co., Inc. (trace elements)
2833 Pennsylvania Street
Allentown, Pa.   18104

Ra-Pid-Gro
88 Ossian Street
Dansville, N.Y.   14437

general supplies

House Plant Corner
Oxford, Md.   21654

Spaeth Displays (topiary forms)
423 W. 55th Street
New York, N.Y.   10019

lighting equipment

Neas Growers Supply Co.
Greenville, S.C. 29604

Shoplite
650 J. Franklin Avenue
Nutley, N.J. 07110

Tube Craft, Inc.
1311 W. 80th Street
Cleveland, Ohio 44102

greenhouses

Aluminum Greenhouses, Inc.
14615 Lorain Avenue
Cleveland, Ohio 44111

Lord and Burnham
Irvington, N.Y. 10533

J. A. Nearing Co., Inc.
10788 Tucker Street
Beltsville, Md. 20705

Riekes Crisa Corporation (glass terrariums)
1818 Leavenworth Street
Omaha, Neb. 68102

Sturdi-built Manufacturing Co.
11304 S.W. Boones Ferry Road
Portland, Ore. 97219

Visual Design Manufacturing Co. (plastic terrariums)
6335 Skyline Drive
Houston, Texas 77027

glossary

annual: a plant that grows from seed to maturity in one season

anther: the pollen-bearing part of the stamen or male reproductive part of the flower

biennial: a plant that grows in two seasons, growing in the first, flowering and setting seed in the second

bract: a small, reduced leaf usually on the stalk of a flower; sometimes, as in poinsettia and dogwood, the bracts are large and showy and mistaken for flowers

bulb: a scaly, usually underground, bud which develops leaves and roots and bears flowers

callus: in a cutting, the new covering of protective tissue

calyx: the outer envelope of the flower, composed of sepals

capsule: a seed pod

catkin: a hanging cluster of petalless flowers

clone: a group of plants identical to each other as a result of vegetative propagation

compound leaf: a leaf composed of two or more leaflets

corm: a solid, bulblike base of a stem such as a crocus corm

cotyledon: a seed leaf evident in large seeds as a bean

cultivar: a cultivated species

deciduous: nonevergreen

dioecious: male and female flowers are borne on different plants

double: flowers that have more than the usual number of petals

downy: covered with soft hairs, as an African violet leaf; also called pubescent

dormant: when a plant is resting or not in active growth

drying-off: a term used for the process of preparing bulbs and tubers for a rest period by withholding water

epiphyte: an air plant

evergreen: a plant that is green year-round

eye: a growing bud on a tuber

forcing: a process of making bulbs bloom out of their normal flowering season; said also of cut stems of trees and shrubs

frond: a leaf of a fern

fruit: the seed-bearing part of a plant

glabrous: not hairy but smooth

glaucous: covered with a white "bloom" that rubs off, as on plums and grapes

graft: a union of one part of a plant (scion) with a root stock

herb: a plant that dies to the ground, especially one with aromatic foliage

herbaceous: not woody; dying down to the ground in late fall

hybrid: a cross resulting from two or more parent plants

internode: the part of the stem between two nodes, growth buds, or leaves

leaflet: a part of a compound leaf

leach: loss of fertilizers and nutrients from the soil by watering

monoecious: male and female flowers borne on the same plant *node:* a joint where leaves or buds appear on a stem

perennial: a plant that lives for three or more years

pinch: to take out the growing tip of a shoot to force branching

petiole: the stem of a leaf

pistil: the female part of the flower

pollen: the male spores of the flower

pot-bound: describes a plant that is in need of re-potting because of excess root growth

propagation: the increasing of plants by seed or vegetative means

pseudobulb: the thickened stem of an orchid plant

pubescent: downy, covered with soft hairs

rhizome: an underground stem containing buds and leaves

runner: a trailing stem that roots, as in Saxifrage

serrate: saw-toothed edges on leaves, as in screw pine

species: a group of like plants forming a subdivision of a genus

stamen: the pollen-bearing portion of the flower

stigma: the part of the pistil that accepts the pollen

stomata: the breathing pores of leaves

stratification: the cold storage of seeds to induce germination

succulent: soft-textured, usually said of leaves

tendril: a twisting extension of a stem by which a plant twines and clings, especially vines such as morning glory

transpiration: the process by which leaves give off moisture through the stomata

tuber: an underground stem with eyes or buds, such as a begonia tuber

turgid: normal leaf state when filled with water

variety: a subdivision of a species; also used to designate a cultivar, or cultivated variety

books on
house plants

Ballard, Ernesta Drinker, *Garden In Your House*. New York, Harper & Brothers, 1971.

Baur, Robert, *Gardens In Glass Containers*. New York, Hearthside Press, 1970.

Brilmayer, Bernice, *All About Begonias*. New York, Doubleday & Company, 1960.

Cherry, Elaine C. *Fluorescent Light Gardening*. Princeton, N.J., D. Van Nostrand Company, 1965.

Chidamian, Claude, *The Book of Cacti and Other Succulents*. New York, Doubleday & Company, 1958.

Crockett, James Underwood, *Flowering House Plants*. New York, Time-Life Encyclopedia of Gardening, 1971.

Crockett, James Underwood, *Foliage House Plants*. New York, Time-Life Encyclopedia of Gardening, 1972.

Cruso, Thalassa, *Making Things Grow*. New York, Alfred A. Knopf, 1969.

Free, Montague, *All About House Plants*. New York, Doubleday & Company, 1946.

Haage, Walther, *Cacti and Succulents*. New York, E. P. Dutton & Company, 1963.

Hersey, Jean, *The Woman's Day Book of House Plants*. New York, Simon & Schuster, 1965.

Kramer, Jack, *Bromeliads*. Princeton, N.J., D. Van Nostrand Company, 1965.

Langer, Richard W., *The After-Dinner Gardening Book*. New York, Collier Books, 1969.

McDonald, Elvin, *The Complete Book of Gardening Under Lights*. New York, Doubleday & Company, 1965.

McDonald, Elvin. *The World Book of House Plants*. Cleveland, World Publishing Company, 1963.

Moore, Harold E. Jr., *African Violets, Gloxinias and Their Relatives*. New York, The Macmillan Company, 1957.

Nehrling, Arno and Irene, *Propagating House Plants*. New York, Hearthside Press, Inc., 1962.

Northern, Rebecca T., *Home Orchid Growing*, 2d. rev. ed. Princeton, N.J., D. Van Nostrand Company, 1965.

Perper, Hazel, *The Avocado Pit Grower's Indoor How-to-Book*. New York, Walker and Company, 1965.

Schulz, Peggie, *All About Geraniums*. New York, Doubleday & Company, 1965.

Sutcliffe, Alys, *House Plants for City Dwellers*. New York, E. P. Dutton & Company, 1964.

Wilson, Helen Van Pelt, *The New Complete Book of African Violets*. New York, M. Burrows and Company, 1963.

latin and common plant names

african evergreen	*syngonium podophyllum*
african pine	*podocarpus*
alligator pear	*persea (avocado)*
alpine violet	*cyclamen*
angel's tears	*helxine*
angel-wings	*caladium*
apple-of-sodom	*solanum sodomaeum*
arrowhead	*syngonium*
arrowroot	*maranta arundinacea*
artillery plant	*pilea microphylla*
australian ivy palm	*brassaia*
australian pine	*araucaria excelsa*
balsam plant	*impatiens*
band plant	*vinca major*
barbados lily	*hippeastrum*
bar-room plant	*aspidistra*
beef plant	*iresine*
belgian evergreen	*dracaena sanderiana*
bermuda buttercup	*oxalis cernua*
bird's nest hemp	*sansevieria hahnii*
blue buttons	*vinca major*
boat lily	*rhoeo discolor*
bog-rosemary	*aeschynanthus*
brain plant	*calathea makoyana*
breadfruit vine	*philodendron pertusum*
brides-bouquet fern	*asparagus plumosus*
busy lizzy	*impatiens sultanii*
cape primrose	*streptocarpus hybridus*
cardinal flower	*rechsteinaria cardinalis*

262

carpet plant	*episcia*
cathedral windows	*calathea makoyana*
cat's claw	*dracaena*
cat tail	*acalypha*
chain cactus	*rhipsalis*
christmas star	*poinsettia*
climbing begonia	*cissus discolor*
clover plant	*oxalis*
corn plant	*dracaena massangeana*
dollar plant	*crassula argentea*
donkey ears	*kalanchoe tomentosa*
elephant's ear	*philodendron domesticum*
emerald feather	*asparagus sprengeri*
fan plant	*begonia rex*
fernleaf aralia	*polyscias filicifolia*
flame nettle	*coleus blumei*
flaming dragon tree	*cordyline terminalis*
friendship plant	*pilea involucrata*
good luck plant	*kalanchoe, oxalis, cordyline*
heart vine	*ceropegia woodii*
honey plant	*hoya imperalis*
hunters robe	*scindapsus aureus*
hurricane plant	*monstera deliciosa*
inch plant	*tradescantia*
irish moss	*helxine soleirolii*
irish shamrock	*oxalis acetosella*
	trifolium dubium
	trifolium repens minus
ivy tree	*fatshedera lizei*
japanese aralia	*fatsia japonica*
lace flower vine	*episcia dianthiflora*
lady's eardrops	*fuchsia*
live-and-die	*mimosa pudica*
lucky plant	*sansevieria trifasciata*
madagascar dragon tree	*dracaena marginata*
mexican breadfruit	*monstera deliciosa*
ming aralia	*polyscias fruticosa*
miniature slipper plant	*sinningia pusilla*
miniature wax plant	*hoya bella*
miracle leaf	*kalanchoe pinnata*
money tree	*crassula argentea*
mother-in-law-plant	*dieffenbachia amoena*
mother-in-law-tongue	*sansevieria trifasciata*
oyster plant	*rhoeo spathacea*
paper flower	*bougainvillea*
parlor ivy	*philodendron oxycardium,*
	senecio mikanoides

patient lucy	*impatiens*
plush plant	*kalanchoe tomentosa*
radiator plant	*peperomia maculosa*
rooting fig	*ficus radicans*
rosary vine	*ceropegia woodii*
royal nodding bells	*streptocarpus wendlandii*
silver heart	*peperomia marmorata*
sky-blue fountain	*streptocarpus hybridus*
small-leaved goldfish vine	*columnea microphylla*
snakeskin plant	*fittonia verschaffeltii*
spider aralia	*dizygotheca elegantissima*
strangler fig	*ficus aurea*
taro vine	*scindapsus aureus*
touch-me-not	*mimosa pudica*
tree of kings	*cordyline terminalis*
tuft root	*dieffenbachia amoena*
wandering sailor	*tradescantia*
white anthurium	*spathiphyllum*
yerba linda	*peperomia rubella*

index

Page numbers in **boldface** refer to the full description of a plant and its culture. Page numbers in *italics* refer to separate illustrations.